Why There Almost Certainly Is a God

Keith Ward

Why There Almost Certainly Is a God

Doubting Dawkins

LION

A Lion Book
an imprint of
Lion Hudson plc
Wilkinson House, Jordan Hill Road,
Oxford OX2 8DR, England
www.lionhudson.com
ISBN 978 0 7459 5330 4 (UK)
ISBN 978 0 8254 7843 7 (US)

Distributed by:
UK: Marston Book Services, PO Box 269, Abingdon, Oxon, OX14 4YN
USA: Trafalgar Square Publishing, 814 N. Franklin Street, Chicago, IL 60610
USA: Christian Market: Kregel Publications, PO Box 2607, Grand Rapids,
Michigan 49501

First edition 2008
10 9 8 7 6 5 4 3 2 1 0

Acknowledgments

Extracts taken from *The God Delusion* by Richard Dawkins published in
the UK and Commonwealth by Bantam Press, 2006, and in the rest of the
world by Mariner Books, 2008. Copyright © 2006 Richard Dawkins.
Permission for UK and Commonwealth granted by Random House.

pp. 29, 64 Scripture quotations taken from the Holy Bible, New International
Version, copyright © 1973, 1978, 1984 International Bible Society. Used by
permission of Zondervan and Hodder & Stoughton Limited. All rights
reserved. The 'NIV' and 'New International Version' trademarks are registered
in the United States Patent and Trademark Office by International Bible
Society. Use of either trademark requires the permission of International
Bible Society. UK trademark number 1448790.

This book has been printed on paper and board independently
certified as having been produced from sustainable forests.

A catalogue record for this book is available
from the British Library

Typeset in 10/14 Bembo
Printed and bound in Wales
by Creative Print and Design

Contents

Preface

In 1991, I was happily living as a Professor of Philosophy at King's College in the University of London when, out of the blue, I received a letter from the office of the Prime Minister, in an official envelope cunningly concealed inside a plain envelope, telling me that the Regius Chair of Divinity at Oxford was vacant, and asking if he could give my name to the Queen. I had not the slightest idea what this meant, and I had to telephone Downing Street to ask how many names the Queen had been given, and what she intended to do with them. It turned out I was being offered the job, and it was an offer I could not refuse.

So I turned up at Oxford, having been transformed by Her Majesty from a philosopher who surprised many people by having some religious beliefs into a theologian who was expected by many people to defend a whole set of religious beliefs as a professional duty. This was a very unexpected change.

When I was a philosopher, and defended belief in God, everyone said, 'How interesting! That is a very original and unusual opinion.' But when I became a theologian, and went on defending the same belief in God, everyone said, 'How boring! That is just what you are paid to say, so you must be some sort of paid church lackey.'

The way I was perceived by other people changed considerably. For some, being a Regius Professor at Oxford (technically, the senior professor in the university) was very grand. But for others, it was a definite slide down the ladder of academic respectability. For from being a free-thinking and radical philosopher, I had suddenly, somewhere on the road from London to Oxford, developed what Richard Dawkins calls a 'theological mind'. And that, he thought, was rather like developing some sort of mental illness.

My arrival in Oxford was heralded by a letter from Richard Dawkins to a public newspaper calling for my resignation, on the ground that there was no such subject as theology, and that I was a particularly stupid example of a theologian anyway.

The reason for his wrath was a short letter I had written to the same newspaper, following a discussion of the Christmas story in the paper. I had written, in what was meant to be a joke, that I knew the three wise men existed because I had seen their tomb in Cologne Cathedral. Admittedly, it was not a very good joke. But it proved too much for Richard Dawkins, who took it as an example of the sort of evidence theologians rely on, and of the best I could do in theological argument.

From that moment, the gloves were off. Even though Dawkins lived and worked in a university with one of the largest and ablest theology faculties in Britain, he went on refusing to admit that there was any such subject as theology. Despite the fact that he and I had entirely friendly and rational personal contacts – as he did with Richard Harries, former Bishop of Oxford, and the vicar of the University Church in Oxford, and the chaplain of his college – he went on proclaiming that all religious believers were stupid, deluded and dangerous. Despite the fact that many Oxford scientists are Christians, and that there is even a Chair in Science and Religion in the university, he went on saying that science and religion were intellectually incompatible. And despite the fact that a number of us have criticized his views publicly many times, he goes on saying that theologians have never answered his arguments.

In fact there has been a series of public debates in Oxford over the last few years, and I do not think it is obvious that he has won them. They have involved, among others, Richard Dawkins and his even more vituperative atheist colleague Peter Atkins on the one side, and myself, Alister McGrath, Richard Harries and Arthur Peacocke on the other.

In recent years, Alister McGrath, a theologian with a doctorate in molecular biology, and John Lennox, Reader in Mathematics at Oxford, have written excellent books responding to Dawkins' arguments. Now it is my turn to rejoin the Oxford God Debate. In a sense, Professor Dawkins got his way – I resigned as Regius Professor of Divinity. But I only did so because I reached retirement age, and I am glad to say that I was succeeded by an eminent medieval philosopher, Marilyn McCord Adams. And though resigned, my pugilistic instincts have not subsided, and I am happy to enter the lists in a head-to-head philosophical confrontation. I am even happier to know that I am bound to win, for when Dawkins talks about theology, he is, on his own admission, talking about a subject that does not exist. It is a traditional definition of Oxford scholars that they know everything about nothing (whereas Cambridge scholars know nothing about everything). So Professor Dawkins stands in a good Oxford tradition. But when a subject does not even exist, there is nothing to know about it. I presume, therefore, that Professor Dawkins actually knows nothing about theology. That gives me a head start. Thus I end my Oxford career, as I began it, with a bad joke. Or could it perhaps be true?

Part 1

On Chapter Two of
The God Delusion

1

The God Hypothesis

A Philosophical Challenge Accepted

The title of this book is the title of Chapter 4 of Professor Richard Dawkins' best-selling *The God Delusion*, with one little difference. I have changed the word 'no' to the word 'a', because I think that change reflects the situation more accurately.

So yes, this is yet another reply to Dawkins by one of those believers in a God whom Dawkins describes as 'arguably the most unpleasant character in all fiction'.[1] My reply will concentrate on Chapters 2 to 4 of Dawkins' book, because those are the chapters in which he enters into the territory of philosophy, of arguments about God and the ultimate nature of reality.

That is my territory. I have taught philosophy in British universities all my working life, and I welcome all comers into that world of clear definitions, sharp arguments and diverse conclusions. Professor Dawkins (I will call him simply Dawkins, for short, and hope it will be taken as a mark of respect and of acknowledgment of his status as a household name) is one of the most exciting and informative writers on science, especially on evolutionary biology. I own all his books. I have learned much from them, and have always been greatly impressed by his capacity to convey the awesomeness of modern science and of the universe it explores.

But when he enters into the world of philosophy, his passion tends to get the better of him, and he sometimes descends into stereotyping, pastiche and mockery, no longer approaching the arguments with his usual seriousness and care. I suspect that he dislikes philosophers, and thinks they are wasting their time sitting around in armchairs instead of carrying out some worthwhile experiments. I often sympathize with him, and regret the fact that I will never make even a half-way decent scientific discovery.

Every now and then, however, I recover my self-respect, and remember that it is important to be critical of all our beliefs – to ask what we mean by them and what reasons there are for accepting them. Philosophy is a systematic attempt to carry out such a process of informed critical enquiry on all our beliefs. In our world, that will involve an enquiry into the nature of science and the nature of religious belief. Whether he likes philosophy or not, Dawkins is doing philosophy in Chapters 2 to 4 of *The God Delusion*. He has come into my world, a world in which I welcome a good argument. In this short book I want to challenge his arguments, to show that they are not at all strong, and to show that there are much stronger arguments in favour of believing in a God – in fact, that it is almost certain that there is a God.

The Spectrum of Philosophical Views of Reality

Dawkins begins by stating the God hypothesis: 'there exists a superhuman, supernatural intelligence who deliberately designed and created the universe and everything in it, including us'.[2] This is one of the few statements he makes about God that I entirely agree with.

The question for discussion, then, is whether the God hypothesis is reasonable and true.

Dawkins advocates an alternative: 'any creative intelligence, of sufficient complexity to design anything, comes into existence only as the end product of an extended process of gradual evolution'.[3] That is a nicely provocative argument that is well worth defending. Oxford is, after all, the home of lost causes, and it is nice to see a cause as lost as this defended.

He has put his finger at once on the central point at issue. Is intelligent mind an ultimate and irreducible feature of reality? Indeed, is it the ultimate nature of reality? Or is mind and consciousness an unforeseen and unintended product of basically material processes of evolution?

If you look at the history of philosophy, it soon becomes clear that almost all the great classical philosophers took the first of these views. Plato, Aristotle, Anselm, Aquinas, Descartes, Leibniz, Spinoza, Locke, Berkeley, Kant, Hegel – they all argued that the ultimate reality, often hidden under the appearances of the material world of time and space, is mind or Spirit.

Even the great philosophical dissenters – most notably David Hume, whose arguments Dawkins often uses, and A. J. Ayer, another great atheist from New College, Oxford – were not materialists. Hume and Ayer thought that the ultimate realities were what they called 'impressions and ideas' or 'sense-data', respectively. These included such things as patches of colour, sounds, touches, smells and tastes. These, they thought, were the primary data, and the world of physical objects and other minds were logical constructs out of them.

This is such a peculiar theory that they often did not believe it themselves, and instead fell back on 'common sense' about what is real. Of course there is a world of enduring physical objects, of course the future will be like the past, of course there are universal laws of nature, of course we are continuing selves who are aware of sense-data, and of course there are other sets of sense-data, in other minds. But none of these things can be proved by argument. They are just common sense beliefs, and we accept them largely because they enable us to navigate our way in a confusing world, because in some sense they 'work'.

Most philosophers in the world have been in some sense idealists — that is, they have thought the ultimate reality is mind. Theists are philosophers who accept this, but add that the physical world does have its own proper reality, which originates from but is different from God, the ultimate mind. An important minority have been phenomenalists, who think that the ultimate reality is the flowing succession of perceptions, thoughts and feelings of which we are aware in immediate experience. From that succession we may construct a world of external physical objects or we may construct the idea of a continuing Self that observes the succession. But in fact there is ultimately only the succession itself. Some forms of Buddhist thought are outstanding examples of this view.

Then there have been common sense philosophers — like Thomas Reid, Hume's contemporary, who was much better known than Hume in his day — who tend to think that human reason is not competent to tell us the truth about ultimate reality. So we must rely on common sense beliefs, a sort of consensus that we accept because it works, or is conducive to survival, health and happiness. Most common sense philosophers have assumed that belief in God is a common sense belief, as it happens.

There have also been scientific realists, like John Locke, who think that there are good arguments for the view that the world consists of colourless clouds of particles in mostly empty space, though we perceive it as a set of coloured solid objects. And there have been sceptics, who do not think that we know anything about the ultimate nature of reality at all, and that even common sense is suspect. But they rarely appear in public, since they are never sure there is any public to whom to appear.

The world of philosophy, of resolute thought about the ultimate nature of things, is a very varied one, and there is no one philosophical view that has the agreement of all competent philosophers. But in this world there are very few materialists, who think we can know that mind is reducible to electrochemical activity in the brain, or is a surprising and unexpected product of purely material processes.

In the world of modern philosophy, there are idealists, theists, phenomenalists, common sense pragmatists, scientific realists, sceptics and materialists. These are all going concerns, living philosophical theories of what is ultimately real. This observation does not settle any arguments. But it puts Dawkins' 'alternative hypothesis' in perspective. He is setting out to defend a very recent, highly contentious, minority philosophical world-view. Good. That is the sort of thing we like to see in philosophy! But it will take a lot of sophisticated argument to make it convincing. It is not at all obvious.

Why Materialism Is Dubious

To most philosophers, materialism has looked like a non-starter. Most of us do not want to deny that material things exist. But we are no longer very sure of what 'matter' is. Is it quarks, or superstrings, or dark energy, or the result of quantum fluctuations in a vacuum? It is certainly not, as the ancient Greek materialist Democritus thought, lumps of hard solid stuff – indivisible atoms – bumping into one another and forming complicated conglomerations that we call people. Some physicists, such as John Gribbin and Paul Davies, in their book *The Matter Myth*,[4] argue that matter is a sort of illusion or appearance produced by some mysterious and unknown substratum in interaction with the human mind.

Quantum physicists such as Bernard d'Espagnat talk about a

'veiled reality' that we can hardly even imagine, which appears as solid physical objects only when observed.[5] And when quantum physicists talk about 'imaginary time' as being more real than 'real time', about the cosmos being a ten- or eleven-dimensional curved space-time, or collection of space-times, and about electrons being probability-waves in Hilbert space, we may well wonder whether matter is a solid foundation for reality after all, or whether we really know what it is.

There is something out there, and it appears to us as a world of fairly solid objects. But modern physics suggests that the nature of reality is very different from what we see, and that it is possibly unimaginable. Roger Penrose, the Oxford mathematician, even thinks that the laws of physics may need to be radically revised, so that they take account of the important role of consciousness in the nature of the world.[6]

What is the point of being a materialist when we are not sure exactly what matter is? It no longer seems to be a set of simple elementary particles. Instead, we have a 'particle zoo' of flickering, insubstantial, virtual wave-particles, most of which (like the elements of dark matter) are probably not detectable by us at all. And it no longer seems that just a few simple laws will account for their behaviour. Instead, we have a very complex mathematics of Hamiltonians, differential equations and Hilbert spaces, which may be elegant and beautiful, but is far from being simple (in the sense of being easy to state and reducible to just one or two basic rules).

What this means is that materialism no longer has the advantage of giving us a simple explanation of reality. Explanations in physics get more and more complicated and counter-intuitive every year. Any plausible form of materialism will be exceedingly complex and mysterious. It no longer has the alleged benefit of being the simplest explanation of the world.

The Problem of Consciousness

When we come to consciousness, things get much worse. The problem of consciousness is so difficult that no one has any idea of how to begin to tackle it, scientifically. What *is* that problem? It is basically the problem of how conscious states – thoughts, feelings, sensations and perceptions – can arise from complex physical brain-states. Even if we are sure that they do arise from brains, we do not know the sorts of connections that conscious states (such as 'seeing a train') have with brain-states (such as 'there is electrical activity at point A in the brain'). We do not know if conscious states can have a causal effect on brain-states, or if they are somehow reducible to brain-states in some way we cannot yet explain.

If Dawkins was a radical materialist, he would state, like his philosophical friend and ally Daniel Dennett, that conscious states are 'nothing more than' brain-states and brain-behaviour. Dennett wrote a book called *Consciousness Explained*,[7] in which he defended this radical theory. Most competent philosophers were unconvinced, and privately referred to his book as 'Consciousness Explained Away'.

The main reason they were unconvinced is that you could very easily have brain-states and behaviour without any conscious states at all. Nobody can observe anyone else's conscious states, and we cannot really be sure that anyone else has any conscious states at all.

The philosopher A. J. Ayer, who was one of the people who tried to teach me philosophy, used to say in seminars that he could not be sure that other people around him had any minds with thoughts in them at all. We did our best to confirm his suspicions. Most of us, however, accept that other people are often thinking, even though we can have no idea of what is going through their minds.

We could attach them to a brain-scanner or put electrodes in their skulls, and record electrical activity and chemical interactions in the brain. But to find out what they are thinking when we do this, we have to ask them. We have not yet got to the stage where we can just attach someone's brain to a recording device and examine their thoughts without asking them to write examination papers, just by measuring electrical activity in their brains.

For many reasons like this, consciousness remains a problem. Few scientifically literate people doubt that human consciousness somehow emerges (we do not know how) from a long, complex evolutionary process. But do we know that no consciousness could exist without being tied to such a physical process? Dawkins' hypothesis says that consciousness 'comes into existence ONLY as the end product' of a long physical process. Further, 'creative intelligences... NECESSARILY arrive late in the universe'.[8] How does he know that? What sort of evidence could there be for thinking that it is absolutely impossible for any form of consciousness to exist except the sort of consciousness that humans have? The most we could say is that we have not come across such a consciousness. All the same, we cannot deny that there might be one. There might be a consciousness that came into existence in some other way. Since we have very little understanding of the ultimate causes of things, it would be hard to rule that possibility out.

The God Hypothesis

The God hypothesis says that there is a consciousness that does not come into being at the end of a long physical process. In fact it does not come into being at all. It did not just spontaneously appear out of nothing. It has always existed, and it always will. There is something that has thoughts, feelings and perceptions, but no physical body or brain. Such thoughts and perceptions will be very different from human thoughts.

To be fair to the God hypothesis, the reality of God is usually said to be infinitely greater than that of any human-like mind that we can imagine. God is not just a projection of a human mind onto the sky. What theistic philosophers usually say is that God is not less than a mind, with consciousness, knowledge and will. The divine reality may be infinitely greater than that, but if we are going to think of it at all, we will not be seriously misled if we think of it as a mind – recognizing that we are using a model suitable for us, but one that does not literally apply to God.

Could there be an unembodied mind, a pure Spirit, that has knowledge and awareness? I can see no reason why not. The God hypothesis has at least as much plausibility as the materialist hypothesis. Both are hard to imagine, but neither seems to be incoherent or self-contradictory. Either might be true.

The existence of consciousness refutes radical materialism, the theory that nothing exists except physical things in space and time. But emergent materialism, the theory that minds arise from matter, even though they are not just material, is more plausible. However, if you are an emergent materialist, you have already taken the first step towards forming some idea of God. You have said that not everything is a physical object in space. There are non-physical, non-spatial entities – minds, perceptions, thoughts and feelings – that really exist, even if they are, as Dawkins claims, causally dependent on physical brains.

Causal dependence is, after all, a contingent matter. It could have been otherwise. Causes could have had quite different effects (the causal laws could have been different), and events could have had quite different causes. Events that are in fact caused might have existed without those causes. So even if minds are in fact caused by a long process of physical development, minds could have existed with a different process of development, or perhaps they could exist without any process of development at all.

This may seem rather odd, but it seems to be a possibility. There could be minds without matter, even if in our actual world finite minds are all causally dependent on specific material causes in our brains. If it is possible for minds to exist without matter, and if God is no less than such an immaterial mind, then God is at the very least a possibility, and not some sort of incoherent 'magic spell', as Dawkins calls God.

Dawkins has a lot of fun with 'supernatural entities', as he calls them. He says that God might exist outside the universe – 'wherever that might be'.[9] That phrase gives his game away. For a materialist, everything that exists is somewhere, in a place, in space. So if God is not in space, Dawkins pretends that he has no idea of where God might be.

The fact is, however, that cosmologists regularly talk, these days, about things outside the universe. They talk about other universes, other space-times, and about sets of quantum laws existing 'outside' space-time. There is really no problem about things existing outside our space-time. And a mind that has no physical body is a very good candidate for something that exists outside (but not, of course, physically outside) any physical space. It exists as pure consciousness.

Believing in God is not at all like believing in fairies or in invisible tea-pots. Those are physical things of a peculiar sort. But God, by definition, is not a physical thing at all, not even a very thin and ghostly physical thing. The question of God is the question of whether conscious mind can exist without any physical body, and whether that mind could account for the origin and nature of our universe. The relatively sensible (emergent) materialist has to admit that this is a possibility.

Arguments for the existence of God are arguments claiming to show that not all minds arise from matter. There is at least one mind that is prior to all matter, that is not in time and therefore is not capable of being brought into being by anything. It is the one truly self-existent reality, and the cause of all physical things.

Obviously such arguments will not work if you simply assume that materialism is true. Then you will see the arguments as starting from a purely physical universe, and magically arriving at God as an extra entity just outside the universe, or snuffling around its boundary, who is made of very thin supernatural matter, and needs just as much explanation as the universe does. That seems to be exactly how Dawkins sees the arguments for God. No wonder he thinks he can dispose of them quite easily!

Arguments for God do not work like that. They are arguments to show that mind is the ultimate reality, and that materialism is a delusion caused by a misuse of modern science. The arguments do not 'prove' that there is one extra pseudo-physical thing in or just outside the universe. They provide good reasons for thinking that the ultimate character of the universe is mind, and that matter is the appearance or manifestation or creation of cosmic mind.

The Recent Rise of Materialism

The rise of materialism in the late twentieth century was undoubtedly due to the enormous success of the physical sciences. Before the sixteenth century, the earth was often thought to be the centre of the universe, and to have existed only for a few thousand years. It was thus easy to think of human consciousness as the central and most important feature of the universe. We are directly aware of thoughts, sensations and feelings, and we construct our view of the physical world, a world of independent material objects, as a sort of inference from our sense-perceptions. However exactly we do that, it did seem sensible at one time to think that the whole universe exists for the sake of human minds.

Since then we have realized that the universe is vastly bigger than this. First of all it was established that the earth is just one planet circling the sun. Then the sun was seen to be just one star among many. Yet even Albert Einstein, when he proposed the Theory of Relativity in 1915, thought that the Milky Way, our galaxy of a hundred billion stars, was the whole of the universe. The Hubble Telescope revealed that the Milky Way is just one of a hundred billion galaxies in the visible universe. And now many cosmologists talk of our whole universe being possibly just one out of billions of other universes.

In addition, we now know that our universe has existed for almost fourteen billion years, and that human beings have only existed for a million or so years at most. In the light of this huge expansion of horizons, it has become impossible to see human minds as the centre of the universe. They exist, it seems, for a tiny flicker of a moment of time in a totally peripheral corner of the universe.

Consciousness has been demoted from being the centre of the universe to being a tiny and very late blip, which probably will not last very long, within a vast and wholly unconscious physical process. Psychologically, that has made materialism seem plausible, or even obviously true, to many people.

In addition, recent advances in brain-science and in computing and artificial intelligence have emphasized the very close dependence of consciousness on the structure and activity of the brain, and the possibility of storing and editing information in complex but purely physical computers. This is so impressive that some scientists have even begun to talk of human minds as information-processing systems, and conscious states begin to seem like superfluous add-ons to our brains, which are information-gathering and processing physical systems.

Despite the psychological impact of these discoveries, they do not change the basic insight of most classical philosophers that consciousness, intellectual understanding and morally responsible action are important and irreducible properties of the real world. However sophisticated computers get, they are not conscious, they do not understand or reflect on the programs that operate on their hardware, and they do not agonize over what moral decisions to make.

I am not denying that some day we may construct a conscious, thinking artificial intelligence. But we are nowhere near that day, and if it comes, we will simply have found a new way of bringing conscious minds into existence. We will not have reduced minds to computers; we will have transformed computers into real minds.

Personal Explanation

Finite minds come into existence when a complex neural network exists. We can formulate a rule that whenever some such neural network exists, then conscious states will exist. But that is a causal statement, not a statement that reduces conscious states to nothing but physical states. If the brain is impaired, our mental processes are impaired, so our mental processes are closely linked to the occurrence of brain-states. But they are still different. We are not just information-processing systems. We are also conscious appreciators of the meaning of information, and creative initiators of new processes of thought.

Those who follow this line of argument will realize that the existence of conscious minds introduces a new form of non-scientific explanation for why things happen as they do. Scientific explanation, in general, works by referring to some initial state (a 'cause') and a general mathematically describable law. That law predicts what regularly follows from the initial state, and it does so without any reference to purpose, value or consciousness.

But there is another sort of explanation. The Oxford philosopher

Richard Swinburne (Dawkins wrongly calls him a theologian, probably because he disagrees with him so much) calls it 'personal explanation'.[10] It only comes into effect when persons, or conscious minds, exist. Then it explains some of the things that persons do in terms of knowledge, desire, intention and enjoyment.

If you want to explain how it is that I am writing these words, you could do so by showing that I am aware of some possible future states (I can stay in bed, have a coffee, or write these words), I evaluate one of them as desirable (I want to finish this book), I set in motion a causal process to bring about what I desire (I get out of bed), and finally I enjoy what I am doing, because it is what I wanted and decided to do.

This is personal explanation. It is a perfectly satisfactory form of explanation, and it does not seem to be reducible to scientific explanation. If it is, no one has yet plausibly suggested any idea of how to reduce it. How can my talk of knowledge, desires, intentions and awareness translate into statements of physics that only refer to physical states and general laws of their behaviour?

I conclude, like most philosophers, that if conscious knowledge, desire, intention and enjoyment exist, then personal explanation is a sort of explanation that we need, one that is truly explanatory, that is quite different from scientific (purely physical) explanation, and that is not reducible to or translatable into scientific explanation.

I do not think Dawkins agrees with this. I was flattered to find myself mentioned in his book, but puzzled when he said, 'Like Swinburne, Ward mistakes what it means to explain something.'[11] However, Swinburne and I are not making a mistake. We are claiming that there is more than one sort of explanation for why things happen as they do. Scientific explanation in terms of physical causes and general laws is one sort of explanation. Personal explanation in terms of desires and intentions is another.

A Final Personal Explanation of the Universe

Of course, personal explanation only comes into play when persons, or fairly sophisticated conscious beings, exist. But on the God hypothesis, there is one conscious mind, the mind of God, which is always in existence. This means that there will be an irreducible personal explanation for why the universe exists. God will know what universes are possible, will evaluate some as more desirable than others, will intend to bring one or more universes about, and will enjoy and appreciate both the activity of bringing them about and the desirable features that God succeeded in bringing about.

If the God hypothesis is true, it is perfectly reasonable to think that God might find the existence of a beautiful, mathematically elegant and intelligible universe desirable. And God might think that it would be good if there were some finite conscious beings that could find the universe desirable too. So we would have a very good personal explanation for why there should be a vast physical cosmos that God could enjoy for its own sake. And we could see that it would be good if that cosmos produced, by a process of long gradual development, conscious beings, parts of the cosmos that could appreciate and enjoy its beauty.

It would not be true that consciousness was an accidental by-product of uncaring physical processes, a peripheral blip on the cosmic screen, soon to be extinguished and forgotten forever. On the contrary, finite conscious beings would be intended by a God who would be aware of their existence forever in the divine mind. So, even if human beings are not the centre of the universe any more, intelligent conscious life would be one central intended purpose of the cosmos. It would not be either accidental or a mere by-product.

The fact that Dawkins does not allow such a form of explanation just shows that he is a materialist. That is fair enough. But he does not admit what a very contentious, unclear and disputed theory materialism is. I do not blame him for that. He is, after all, arguing a rhetorical case. Nevertheless, it is only fair to point out that there are things he systematically neglects to mention, but that a great many philosophers, both dead and alive, accept. Two big ones are: the irreducible existence of consciousness, and the irreducible nature of personal explanation.

It is very unsatisfactory to have two different sorts of explanation, with no obvious way of connecting them in one coherent scheme of thought. The materialist hypothesis tries to connect them either by reducing the personal to the physical (reductive materialism), or by supposing that the personal just emerges out of the physical for no particular reason (emergent or non-reductive materialism). The former theory conflicts with our everyday experience of conscious life. The latter gives up on explanation.

The God hypothesis connects personal and scientific explanation by postulating that there is an overarching cosmic personal explanation that explains physical states and laws as means to realizing some envisaged purpose. This, I think, seems a very elegant solution. But it does require an explanation of why God, the cosmic mind, exists. Dawkins thinks such an explanation cannot be found. 'The laws of probability forbid all notions of their [intelligent conscious beings like God] spontaneously appearing without simpler antecedents.'[12] I will return to this point later, but here will just issue a reminder that God does not spontaneously appear. God, being timeless, either always is or never is. It is not at all clear that the laws of probability, which properly apply to things in this universe, have anything to say about the likelihood of timeless and immaterial conscious intelligences. But there is more to be said on this matter, and in due course I will say it.

Is the Existence of God a Scientific Hypothesis?

For the moment, it is easy to see that the God hypothesis and the materialist hypothesis clash head-on. The debate is not primarily about whether the physical universe needs a designing intelligence to explain why it exists. It is about whether the physical universe really is the ultimate reality, or whether the ultimate reality has the nature of mind or consciousness. Arguments for God do not agree with materialism for 95 per cent of the time, and then at the last moment introduce a designer to account for the complex arrangements of matter. Arguments for God disagree with materialism at the very first step, the step of saying that matter has independent, solid, obvious reality.

Dawkins fails to see this. Or, more likely, he sees it but refuses to admit it because it does not suit his highly rhetorical purpose. So he says that 'the existence of God is a scientific hypothesis like any other'.[13] Of course, he really knows this is not true. He is setting a trap for theists, to try to get them to accept materialism without realizing quite what they are doing. He does that very cleverly, as one would expect. But it is very easy to show that he is wrong.

There are many sorts of science, ranging from ethology (the study of animal behaviour in the wild) and botany to mathematical cosmology. Ethologists place a high value on careful and sustained observation, on experimental testing of hypotheses wherever possible, and on the framing of hypotheses that can explain, and to some extent predict, animal behaviour. Cosmology is much more abstract. Its observations have a more indirect, but still vital, relation to the mathematical models by which they seek to explain the origin and development of the cosmos.

In most sciences, from the mainly observed to the most speculative, there is a strong emphasis on public observations that are repeatable, in principle, that usually give rise to some specific predictions, and that can be tested under controlled conditions. If a hypothesis cannot be tested under specifiable conditions, it is not a scientific hypothesis.

There are lots of hypotheses that are not scientific. For instance, most of the hypotheses made by historians are not scientific. When a historian explains the origins of the First World War by reference to a set of economic and social factors, and the motives and ambitions of politicians, that historian is making a hypothesis. The hypothesis may be more or less convincing or plausible. But it certainly gives rise to no predictions about the future, the conditions it talks about cannot be repeated or controlled, and the hypothesis cannot be proved by any set of public observations. Many historical accounts involve attributions of motives, desires and intentions to long-dead people. There is an ineliminable element of subjective interpretation involved in such attributions, and that is precisely what makes history interesting. But it is also what makes history a subject that appeals to personal explanation, and not to purely scientific explanation. History is not a natural science, but it is none the worse for that.

There are thousands of other factual hypotheses that are not scientific. If I suppose that I had a dream last night, there is no way of publicly observing my dream, of repeating it, or of making predictions as a result of it. Brain activity during sleep is subject to scientific confirmation. But the content of my dreams is not – and I might know that there is such content though I will never reveal it to anyone, and will probably forget it myself in a few days. That I actually had dreams last night is a hypothesis that is factual but not scientific. We do not need to appeal to dreams for examples of factual but non-scientific hypotheses. If I suppose that I will meet you for coffee tomorrow, that is certainly a factual prediction that will be verified or disconfirmed in due course. But it is not a scientific hypothesis.

The God hypothesis is neither scientific nor historical, nor does it just provide a record or prediction of my subjective experiences. It does not give rise to specific predictions, and it cannot be tested by public observation in controlled conditions. It does not make factual claims that will be conclusively verified by all concerned in the near future.

It is a philosophical or metaphysical hypothesis. It proposes that the reality in which we live can be best understood by postulating one kind of reality as ultimate, and as accounting for all the rich array of realities that we seem ourselves to experience. As we have seen, there are many different metaphysical hypotheses. Arguments between them cannot be resolved by observation or experiment. That is why they are not scientific.

Can We Establish by Science That God Exists?

Observations and experiments are nevertheless relevant to establishing the truth or plausibility of metaphysical hypotheses. If there are no events at all that could reasonably be taken as revealing the presence of God, then the God hypothesis is less probable. If prayers were never felt to be answered, the hypothesis that God answers prayer would be much less probable.

As Dawkins rightly says, 'A universe with a supernaturally intelligent creator is a very different kind of universe from one without.'[14] However, he also admits that 'it may not be so easy in practice to distinguish one kind of universe from the other'.[15]

A universe without God might well be a universe without any general and reliable laws of nature. It would have no purpose and no objective morality or moral goal. It might be without any conscious life, morally responsible agents, or beings that could understand and appreciate the beauty and intelligibility of nature. In such a world there would be no intelligent agents, no miracles, no divine revelation and no providential direction of history. There would be no immortality and no apprehensions of the divine in art, morality, nature, or in contemplative prayer. A theist would add, of course, that without God there would be no universe at all!

But things are a bit more complicated than this. There could be a universe without God that had reliable laws of nature, even a 'purpose' of sorts (in the sense of a direction of evolution towards greater complexity), an objective morality, conscious life, responsible agents, and even a strong appearance of design (really caused by blind natural selection, of course). Dawkins thinks the universe is like that, anyway. The atheistic universe could even be filled with beings who thought there were miracles, answers to prayer and providential guidance. After all, as Dawkins says, the human brain is capable of almost anything.

The universe could look as though it were intelligently designed, filled with miracles, revelations and experiences of God, and with intimations of moral obligation and purpose. And yet there might not be a God. So in what way is God a scientific, testable hypothesis? There are even very good reasons why God might not be subject to scientific experiment. The Bible says, 'Do not put the Lord your God to the test' (Luke 4:12). That seems to rule out experimenting on God. And that seems right, since we would not even experiment on our friends and loved ones, to find out, for example, if they really loved us. There would be something deeply wrong with such a thing.

So it seems that God does make a difference, but it is not a neutrally testable difference that could be settled by experiment. Dawkins' suggestion that the resurrection of Jesus is 'a strictly scientific question' is truly mind-boggling, and he must be saying it tongue firmly in cheek. Of course it is a question of fact, of what actually happened in history. But there is no way of directly confirming that history now by personal experience of it. It is a historical, not a scientific, question. And it concerns the experiences of a group of long-dead people, the disciples of Jesus. The judgment as to whether or not the resurrection happened as recorded in the Bible is likely to depend on whether or not you already believe in God. It is not public evidence for God. It would confirm belief in a God of a certain kind if we also already accepted, or if we were open to the possibility of, a set of beliefs that made such a divine action plausible.

The most significant of those beliefs is the belief that the ultimate reality is the divine consciousness. If you held that belief, the plausibility of a testimony to the resurrection would be greatly enhanced. But it would still not be evidence in the scientific sense of proving beyond all reasonable doubt that there was a divine being who was liable to act in predictable resurrecting ways when the circumstances were right.

I conclude that the question of God is certainly a factual one, but certainly not a scientific one. It lies at the very deep level of ultimate metaphysical options. So while evidence can be marshalled for or against it, it will never be conclusively settled, either for or against. Different interpretations of the same data will always be possible. The question is which fundamental interpretation is most adequate. I have no doubt that the God hypothesis is wholly reasonable and powerful, even if it is not true. But I also think that the God hypothesis *is* true, and more reasonable than its main competitor, the materialist hypothesis. As I move on to consider Dawkins' treatment of the 'arguments for God', I will show why this is the case.

Part 2

On Chapter Four of *The God Delusion*

2

Large Aeroplanes and God

The Boeing 747 Gambit

I will begin my discussion of arguments for the existence of God with what Dawkins calls 'the big one', or the argument from improbability. He undertakes to give a statistical demonstration that God almost certainly does not exist. Dawkins calls it the 'ultimate Boeing 747 gambit' and he thinks it comes close to proving that God does not exist. He says it is an argument 'to which I have yet to hear a theologian give a convincing answer'.[1] Well, here it is!

Right at the start a note of caution is needed. Dawkins speaks of a 'statistical demonstration'. Yet just a few pages earlier he had (rightly, in my view) dismissed an argument in favour of God that relied on giving numerical values to various probabilities, and then by calculating all those probabilities, arriving at an overall value for the probability of God.

The trouble with such arguments, he said, is that the probabilities are not exactly measurable quantities. They are very personal judgments of how probable you think things are. And, he says, 'who cares about subjective judgments?'[2] Yes, indeed. We need to ask the question of whether Dawkins' assignment of 'statistical probabilities' to the question of God is not also just a subjective judgment. I rather think it is, and that it is well-nigh impossible to give precise numerical values to the probability of things like God existing. Dawkins' argument might well be more subjective and personal than he claims it is. We shall see.

The argument Dawkins provides is called the Boeing 747 gambit because of a remark allegedly made by astronomer Fred Hoyle that the probability of life originating on earth by chance is no greater than the chance that a hurricane, blowing through a scrap yard, would assemble a Boeing 747. Dawkins' argument is that it is indeed hugely improbable that such a complex machine could suddenly appear by chance. But the complex organisms of present-day life on earth have not appeared spontaneously or by chance. They have gradually assembled piece by piece by the mechanisms of random mutation and natural selection. 'Each of the small pieces is slightly improbable',[3] so there is a long process of slight improbabilities which builds up to something that looks immensely improbable, but is not.

Moreover, 'a designer God cannot be used to explain organized complexity because any God capable of designing anything would have to be complex enough to demand the same kind of explanation in his own right'.[4] God would be the ultimate Boeing 747, and his existence would be even more difficult to explain than an aeroplane spontaneously assembled in a scrap yard.

Evolution and Intelligent Creation

Evolution, on Dawkins' account, is not purely random. It works by two major mechanisms: replication with random mutation, and selection for survival by the environment. This is not just a random shuffle. Mutations in DNA are called 'random' because they are not all directed towards improving organisms, but have both good and bad effects on the organisms constructed on DNA recipes. But they are not completely random, because they occur in accordance with general laws of physics which, considered in enough detail, might make the mutations that occur at least probabilistically predictable.

If those laws of physics are going to be roughly what they are, then as a strand of DNA unravels and copies itself, there are going to be small variations in the copied strands that form the basis for heredity. Zoologist Matt Ridley estimates that there are about a hundred variations – mutations – in each human generation.[5] It is quite possible that the sorts of mutations that get preserved and passed on to future generations can be predicted in general. Harmful changes will be wiped out and adaptive changes will replicate better, and it may be possible to predict what sorts of changes will happen, given enough time and an environment whose general character is reasonably stable.

This is actually a matter of some controversy among evolutionary biologists. No one denies that mutations happen in accordance with the laws of nature, but there is much dispute about whether the sorts of mutations that are adaptive can be predicted, or indeed whether any adaptive mutations could be expected to occur at all. The American biologist Stephen J. Gould, as is well known, held that if we ran the tape of evolution on earth over again, we would get quite a different result.[6] This is a strong sense of 'chance', which supposes that no complex life-forms may evolve, or that if they do, they may take a whole host of different forms, very unlike humans, for example.

As I understand him, Dawkins disagrees with this view, though I do not think he goes as far as Simon Conway Morris, Professor of Evolutionary Palaeontology at Cambridge University, who postulates that, given the fundamental laws of physics, the structure of carbon, and so on, even the development of carbon-based life-forms is inevitable, in the right environment.[7]

Still, I think Richard Dawkins takes the evolution of some sort of complex life-form to be more or less inevitable, given the basic laws of physics. Mutations that have no particular direction in themselves, nevertheless, given their selection by the environment, will inevitably take the direction of greater complexity, and even intelligence may be predictable as a beneficial survival strategy, if life is not exterminated too soon by some cosmic catastrophe such as a collision with an asteroid.

I think this Darwinian story is immensely illuminating, and Dawkins tells it very well. But he does not quite bring out how controversial, within evolutionary biology, is the view that the whole process is more or less bound to happen, somewhere or other in the universe.

He also neglects to mention that his view is much more compatible with theism than is the view of biologists such as Gould. It is difficult to think of a God who creates the universe for a purpose, yet leaves the outcome completely to chance – in which case the divine purpose might never get realized. But it is easy to think that an intelligent God might set up the basic laws of nature so that intelligent life would inevitably result. Dawkins' view of the laws of evolution is not really very different from that of many theists. Except, of course, that he denies any possibility of supernatural 'intervention' in, or causal interaction with, the process. And he thinks that God is a superfluous addition to the causal process.

God would not be superfluous, however, if God explained just why the laws of nature are as life-conducive as they actually are. The explanation would be what I have called a personal explanation – the laws are chosen by God precisely in order to generate intelligent life. If that is so, the existence of a designing God would certainly raise the probability of the laws of nature being such as to lead to the existence of intelligent life. It would make the existence of such laws virtually certain. So the God hypothesis is not superfluous after all. It is a very good explanation.

The Evolution Program

It does seem to be immensely improbable that this whole set-up should exist — that is, general laws that cause subatomic particles to assemble into fairly stable atoms, which in turn assemble into long complicated self-replicating molecules, which form codes for assembling proteins into organic bodies that replicate and become, over time, increasingly well adapted to their environment, so that hugely intricate and complex organisms live and reproduce — just as a result of the operation of a few general laws and a set of simple subatomic particles.

Dawkins invented a neat computer game, which he called 'the Evolution program', to illustrate the process.[8] He showed how a repeated process of generating geometrical shapes by the application of a few suitably chosen laws, together with a little judicious selection (he repeatedly selected the shapes upon which the process would continue to operate in order to produce the sorts of shapes he wanted), could eventually produce very interesting and insect-like patterns.

The point is that you can get organized complexity by random mutation, as long as you have the right set of basic laws of recombination and selection. Of course, Dawkins wants to show that this can all happen without any conscious selection. In real life, he says, the selecting is done by the entirely natural and repeated selection of short-term outcomes that have greater reproductive success. By a long series of such 'selections', organized complexity will, perhaps inevitably, result.

But he admits, I think, that it takes a very special set of initial laws to achieve such a result. And, although he insists that there is no goal or purpose in the process, if some intelligent creator did have the purpose of producing intelligent carbon-based life by a gradual process of ever-more complex physical structures, the evolutionary process is an excellent way to achieve that purpose.

We do not need an intelligent creator, he says. Blind and gradual selection will do the trick. Well, it may, and I do not deny it. But the chances of it doing so, given all the alternative paths of evolution there are, still seem to be astronomically small. Unless, that is, the laws governing the sorts of mutation that occur have been carefully worked out beforehand.

It is not true that the postulate of an intelligent creator is superfluous. For such a creator would raise the probability that the process would result in intelligent life by an enormous amount. In fact it would make it virtually certain, as opposed to being just one possibility among countless others. That might not give us any new biological information, so it might be superfluous to scientific understanding. But it would not be superfluous to philosophical understanding, for which it is reasonable to accept a hypothesis that raises the probability that the world should be as it is.

After all, Dawkins spent quite a lot of time working out just what the laws had to be to produce the result he wanted. The Evolution program took a great deal of very intelligent design. And the program had a desired goal – it would never have existed otherwise. It was not the computer or the program that envisaged the goal. It was the intelligent designer.

What is the moral? The moral is that it takes a very intelligent being to devise a set of laws and a suitable environment (with the right degree of oxygen and nitrogen, the right distance from a star and the right protection from the most destructive cosmic debris) to produce a process that will result in the origin of complex replicating organisms.

So it would seem, in any case, and I think Dawkins would agree that it *looks* that way. But, he argues, there is in fact no goal or purpose for our universe. It will all inevitably end in the cold darkness of a universe expanded inexorably into emptiness. And the appearance of intelligent design can easily be accounted for, he says, by the Darwinian mechanisms of replication, modification and natural selection. That is precisely the force of the Darwin algorithm. It eliminates the attraction of positing an intelligent designer of the system who, Dawkins repeatedly says, would have to be even more complex than the system it is supposed to explain.

The New Argument for Design

Yet a hesitation remains. The laws might so easily have been slightly different, the environmental conditions could so easily have inhibited the existence of any complex molecules, and the genetic mutations could so easily have been too fragile and chaotic to keep stable basic structures in existence. That is why the whole process is still hugely improbable. It is improbable, given the possible range of alternatives – different constants of gravity, different values of the strong and weak nuclear forces, different planetary conditions – that could equally easily have existed.

Even Simon Conway Morris, who believes that carbon-based organisms are inevitable given the basic laws of physics, thinks that the existence of a planet on which such organisms could thrive is so improbable that it may have only happened once in the whole history of the universe.

So I think that Dawkins is not correct when he claims that appeal to the Darwin algorithm completely destroys the argument from improbability. Darwin does explain (make more probable) the existence of complex organisms by processes of replication, modification and selection operating on simpler parts. But Darwin does not explain just why those processes and the laws on which they are based are as effective as they are. Darwin's theory does not make probable the existence of those laws, when there seem to be a great many alternatives to their being as they are.

Darwin felt this difficulty strongly. Darwin said, in the *Origin of Species*, 'How infinitely complex and close-fitting are the mutual relations of all organic beings.'[9] And again, in a letter, he wrote, 'I cannot persuade myself that electricity acts, that the tree grows, that man aspires to the loftiest conceptions, all from blind, brute force.'[10]

Dawkins may protest that it is not all blind, brute force. But that would obscure the issue here. He himself coined the expression 'The Blind Watchmaker'. Nature is blind, in that it does not foresee or plan what will occur in the future. It is brute force, in that it cares nothing for the fate of human beings or for their well-being.

When Dawkins says that natural selection is not random, he just means that, given an ecosystem of a specific sort, it will follow that specific sorts of organisms will prove to be adaptive. He writes, 'We can safely predict that, if we wait another ten million years, a whole new set of species will be as well adapted to their ways of life as today's species are to theirs.'[11] But this is a very controversial claim. The earth might have been destroyed long before that. Or strands of DNA may, for some reason, just stop replicating at all, decomposing into pools of chemicals. Or the mutations that occur may fail to produce the stable structures with relatively gentle modifications that are necessary to enable cumulative selection and adaptation to occur.

There is any number of ways in which the Darwinian process of slow, gradual, cumulative adaptation could fail. This is not an argument for God. But it shows that reliance on the predictability of nature, and on its tendency to produce increasingly complex and adapted organic life-forms, is dependent on a very specific adjustment of physical laws that is itself hugely improbable.

The design argument, in its seventeenth-century form – finding the existence of organic life-forms to be too improbable to have arisen spontaneously by chance – may have been superseded by Darwin. But the design argument still lives, as an argument that the precise structure of laws and constants that seem uniquely fitted to produce life by the process of evolution is hugely improbable. The existence of a designer or creator God would make it much less improbable. That is the New Design Argument, and it is very effective.

The Search for a Deeper Explanation

If you ask whether the process of evolution, as we see it, is hugely improbable, the answer is 'yes'. The laws of nature could have been different. There might have been no habitable planet circling a star that was not either too hot or too cold. There might have been no origin of life. There might have been no cumulative build-up of complex replicating molecules. There might have been no environment stable enough to allow the long, slow process of organic formation to take place. There might have been no formation of eucaryotic cells, the very complex cells that are the basis of animal organisms. There might never have been consciousness or intelligence. It is because the set of 'might-have-beens' is so immensely long that the existence of intelligent life on this planet seems so immensely improbable.

The argument from improbability does not state, as Dawkins says it does, 'that complex things *could not have* come about by chance'. That is too strong. There are two rather different meanings of the expression 'by chance'. In the strongest sense, it means that things come into existence without any cause or reason. Scientists usually discount this possibility, and accept as a basic assumption that every change has some cause or reason.

In the rather weaker sense, coming about 'by chance' means

by a random shuffling of possible states of a physical system. Using this weaker sense, the argument from improbability states that it is almost unimaginably improbable that complex things like human beings came about by chance. The unimaginably improbable can happen. Perhaps it has! But the point is this: anything that makes the process less improbable is an improvement. It is something every good scientist would want. A good scientific theory is good largely because it makes an improbable process more probable.

That is why Darwinism, whether it ultimately turns out to be true or not, is a good scientific theory: it makes the existence of the different life-forms on our planet – together with many structural similarities between them, and with many peculiar 'faults' that would be hard to account for as specifically designed – more probable than a non-evolutionary theory that says they all just came into existence at once, or by a random shuffling of elementary particles.

I agree with Dawkins that Darwinism is a good explanation of why living forms are as they are. It is superior to any theory that living forms just originated by chance, without any process of replication, modification and cumulative selection. When Dawkins writes on this topic, he does so supremely well. But having said that, the whole amazing process of evolution is still hugely improbable, in the light of all the possible alternative processes there might have been. As Dawkins argues elegantly, given the basic laws of nature and a long, gradual process of cumulative mutation and selection, the improbability of the complex integrated organisms we see around us on earth is much reduced. Yet the existence of precisely those laws, out of all the other ones that might have existed, and the very rare environmental conditions that allow cumulatively complex organisms to form, still seems very improbable.

So it would be good, scientifically, if we could get behind the Darwinian explanation, and in some way make the existence of those laws, with their very precise and correlated values, more probable. Evolutionary theory leads to a search for a deeper level of explanation, an explanation that would raise the probability of the laws, forces and structures of nature being as they are.

Is the Simple More Probable Than the Complex?

Part 1: Wholes and Parts

My argument so far has been that, while Darwinism is a good explanatory theory, it is not a final theory. The process of evolution may not be due to chance; it may even be inevitable, given the basic laws of nature. But that the laws of nature should be as they are, when there are so many possible alternatives, is now where improbability is located. It would be good if we could find some way of reducing that improbability. Darwin has not finally satisfied our intellectual curiosity. One very good candidate for a final explanation is the existence of God, who could ensure that the laws of nature were just right for the evolution of intelligent life.

But Dawkins thinks he has a conclusive rebuttal of God. God, he says, must be just as complex as the reality that God is supposed to create. So God is at least as improbable as the laws of nature themselves. In fact, God must be more improbable than anything in the physical universe: 'Any entity capable of intelligently designing something as improbable as... a universe would have to be even more improbable.'[12] Dawkins goes even further: 'Any God capable of designing a universe... must be a supremely complex and improbable entity.'[13] God is supremely improbable, so improbable that hardly anything could be less probable. Therefore God is not a final explanation at all, because God needs explanation even more than the laws of nature do.

An important premise in this argument is that complex entities are less probable than simple entities. So God, a very complex entity, is less probable than something like a set of simple elementary particles and laws. And it is useless to explain the more probable in terms of the less probable. But is it true that complex entities are less probable than simple ones?

First of all we need to define what is meant by 'simple' and 'complex'. These words have many different meanings, and it will be confusing to run those different meanings together. We need to separate them out. One sense of 'simple' is the fairly obvious, but still important, one that parts of a whole are simpler than the whole. Since physical wholes are made of physical parts, it seems that the existence of a very complex whole is less simple than the separate existence of its parts. This may seem to entail that a complex whole is less probable than the existence of one of its simple parts. That is because there are many possible combinations of parts. If there are one thousand parts in a given whole, then the chance of them being assembled in any particular way is very small indeed, given the thousands of different ways in which they could be arranged. There are billions of atoms in a human body. So the chance of their existing in the highly complex and integrated form they take is very small indeed.

But I have noted, and Dawkins certainly agrees, that there may be laws that entail the combination of parts into wholes. In that case, complex wholes would not be less probable than their parts, but just as probable – perhaps even certain, given the nature of the parts and the basic laws governing their combination.

If we look at a complex eye, we may wonder how atoms could assemble into such a very complex whole of interacting parts, and think it very unlikely it would happen by random shuffling. But if there are laws of nature that dictate the combination of atoms into assemblies of molecules, then we are no longer speaking of random shuffling. We are speaking of events entailed by laws, and of events that may cumulatively and gradually build into more complex unities in a natural way – this is what Dawkins calls going round the back of Mount Improbable. The eye, though wonderful, will no longer be unlikely; it may be an inevitable outcome of the laws of physics and chemistry and biology. The laws explain the eye by making its existence probable.

The Darwinian laws of replication, modification and selection are consequences of some of the more basic laws of nature, so of course they also explain by making what seems unlikely appear to be rather likely. Dawkins repeatedly emphasizes this point, and he does so very well.

But if the existence of complex organs such as eyes is actually made highly probable by the basic laws of nature, then it is not, after all, obvious that the simple is more probable than the complex.

The introduction of laws of nature shows how simples may inevitably build into complexes, and may – as Conway Morris argues – even generate intelligent life as a necessity. Wholes are made of parts, and so they depend on the existence of parts. But they also depend on the existence of laws of nature, and so they may not be less probable than their parts. Whether they are less probable will depend on how many possible alternatives to a given complex the laws of nature allow.

In our universe, it looks as though the formation of complex molecules of DNA, while a natural outcome of fundamental laws of physics, depends on the existence of many fortuitous conditions. That makes them seem improbable. But if physical laws make the processes of nature necessary, we might see that in fact the formation of life on earth was absolutely necessary. It all depends on how tightly determining the laws of nature are.

I conclude that the simple is not, as such, more probable than the complex. It is only so in the special circumstance that there is a very complex arrangement of parts, when those parts could easily have been arranged in many different ways. But once you introduce laws of nature, those alternative possibilities may disappear. Then the complex is no longer highly improbable.

Part 2: On the Probability of Universes

It would still, however, be highly improbable in our universe to find that a complex whole existed in the absence of any laws of nature or process of generation. That is because the parts could have been arranged in many different ways. If we know the number of those ways, we can assess the probability exactly. With a very complex whole, the probability is very small.

Is the probability of simple parts existing any smaller than the probability of complex parts existing? Dawkins seems to think that the existence of simple parts is only 'slightly improbable',[14] whereas the existence of a complex whole is very improbable indeed. But in this he is almost certainly wrong.

What he probably has in mind is that if you think of the spin of an electron, there are only two possible states the electron could be in – 'spin up' and 'spin down'. If an electron only has two possible states, then the probability of its being in one of those states is fifty–fifty. That is not improbable at all.

Now if you think of a very complex whole, like a molecule of DNA, with millions of component parts, there are clearly even more millions of alternative orderings of those component parts that could exist. So the probability of one of those orders of parts existing is only one in a few million. That is very improbable indeed.

Obviously, it might seem, the complex DNA molecule is much more improbable than the simple electron. This seems to support Dawkins' view that simple states are much less improbable than complex states.

But we need to think again. What we have just done is to try to compare the probabilities of the occurrence of two different states of affairs, given quite a lot of background information about actual laws of nature and actually existing states of affairs. First of all we assume that electrons exist, and that 'spin' is a property that electrons have. Given that fact, we try to assess the probability of a particular electron having a specific spin. It is fifty per cent. Then we assume that DNA molecules exist, and that they are made up of a huge number of parts. If we assume that these parts are just randomly ordered, the probability of DNA molecules having a specific ordering of parts is infinitesimal.

But, of course, this is the wrong assumption. There is a past history of evolving development, and the likelihood of intrinsic correlations that very often afford an explanation of how that particular configuration was found (this is Dawkins' argument in *Climbing Mount Improbable*). Without that essential background information, our estimate of probability could be completely erroneous. More is involved in a true calculation than simple combinations of uncorrelated factors. Even so, the probability of a specific ordering of the parts of a large molecule is much smaller than the probability of an electron having 'spin up' or 'spin down'. The simple state looks more probable than the complex state.

But suppose we have no background information about the existence and properties of electrons, or of large molecules, or about the laws of nature. Suppose there are no laws of nature and no actual states of affairs at all. What could we then say about the probability of there being such things as electrons or large complex molecules?

The truth is that we could say nothing at all about it. In desperation, we might try to list all the possible states of affairs there could possibly be, and decide how probable it is that any one of them might exist. But this seems a forlorn hope. How do we know how many possible states of affairs there are, or how to assign numerical probabilities to them?

If we do not know how to begin assigning probabilities when there are no actual existents or laws of frequency that could be discovered, we are forced to the conclusion that we cannot make judgments of probability at all. And if that is the case, then we cannot say that it is more probable that simple states of affairs will exist than that complex states will exist.

It might even be said that, since there are presumably many more complex possible states than simple ones, then if every state has exactly the same probability of existence as every other state, taken as a whole it is rather more likely that any state that exists will come from the much larger sub-class of complex states. The complex will be more probable than the simple!

But I think it is better to say that this sort of probability calculation is just impossible in principle. There are no grounds for speaking of the probabilities of the existence of the various states, when there are no actual background data to refer to. So there are no grounds for saying that simple things are either more or less likely to exist than complex things.

It is not true to say, as Dawkins does, that 'the laws of probability forbid the existence of intelligence without simpler antecedents'.[15] The laws of probability forbid nothing of the sort. It is the laws of the nature of our actual universe that forbid such a thing. And they certainly do not forbid it absolutely. They forbid it only for finite intelligences in this space–time. The laws of probability either have nothing to say about the existence of God, or they will say that God is not more improbable than the existence of a few simple electrons (if electrons are really all that simple, which seems highly unlikely). Moreover, you cannot say, in a situation where there are no actual states, entities, laws or properties, that a simple state is more likely to exist than a complex state. You cannot say anything very illuminating at all. The laws of probability are just not going to apply.

Three Senses in Which God Is Simple, and in Which the God Hypothesis Is Elegant, Economical and Comprehensive

So far I have accepted that God is complex, in the obvious sense that God's mind contains the ideas of all possible states of affairs, and that God is capable of all possible actions that are compatible with the divine nature. I have also proved that the existence of such a complex God is not less probable than the existence of a universe of simple elementary particles and laws.

But actually it can be very misleading just to say that God is complex, and leave it at that. For there are other important senses of 'simple' and 'complex' that need to be considered.

In traditional religious thought there are three important senses in which God is said to be simple. The first is that God is not complex in the sense of being composed of separate and separable parts. The ideas in God's mind are not separately existing ideas that are added together to form the mind of God. They only exist as part of the mind of God, which is one consciousness. It is not possible to take some separate ideas and build them up into a mind that contains them. The mind comes first, and its ideas are parts that are inseparable from that mind. The ideas cannot be taken out and made parts of another mind. It is the unity that comes first, and the 'parts' only exist as part of that unity. In this sense, God is simple in a way that no physical thing is simple, because physical things are made of smaller, separable parts.

Secondly, God is simple in the sense in which a being that acts on one or two general principles is simpler than a being that acts on many different and changing principles. The simplest sort of mind is a mind that does not consist of many arbitrarily linked and contingent elements. It is a mind that is wholly rational and intelligible, and that acts on principles that are consistent and reliable. God is simple in this second sense, of being a mind that works on elegant, perspicacious and rational principles.

The God hypothesis posits that there is a mind that knows all possible states. It can distinguish between good and bad (rationally desirable and undesirable) states. If it acts, it will do so in order to realize and enjoy good states. And it will obviously choose the best possible states for itself, so that it will be supremely good (again, in the sense of being supremely desirable for its own sake). This hypothesis is the basis of the final personal explanation of the universe that is postulated by theism.

It follows that, on this hypothesis, God acts on just one fundamental principle, the principle of creating for the sake of goodness. That is the simplest and most comprehensive principle there could be. And God knows, not by happening to gather information from many external sources, but by knowing the divine nature itself, with the ideas of all possible states of being that it contains, and by knowing all actual states as the products of its own action.

Thus God knows by one intellectual act – knowledge of the divine nature itself. God acts on one general principle – for the sake of goodness. These two principles are united in one deeper principle, because knowledge of the divine nature is knowledge of the supremely good, and acting for the sake of goodness entails knowing all that is good. So God's one ultimate, simple intellectual act is the knowledge and choice of goodness for its own sake. This is the simplest and most comprehensive sort of mind there could be. It causes and comprehends all reality in the simplest possible intellectual operation.

A third sense in which God is simple is that God is the one and only cause of all existence except the divine existence itself, which can have no cause. This is the sense often described as Occam's Razor – 'do not multiply entities unnecessarily'. On this principle, God is just one entity, whereas if you have lots of elementary particles and laws, or even lots of universes, you have many entities. You then need to ask whether they are really necessary.

I have shown that the simple is not, as such, more probable than the complex. Nevertheless, it is aesthetically pleasing to find that the idea of God, of one (simple, sense three) indivisible (simple, sense one) mind, acting on one general principle (simple, sense two), is more economical and elegant than the idea, preferred by materialists, of an undefined number of material elements and laws.

Not only is the God hypothesis just as probable as the materialist hypothesis. It is more economical and elegant, and it is more comprehensive, since it succeeds in accounting for purpose and value in the universe as well as for the existence of physical entities in a way that the materialist hypothesis cannot. That makes it a very attractive hypothesis. When Dawkins writes of me that I 'seem not to understand what it means to say of something that it is simple',[16] he has overlooked the different meanings that the term 'simple' has. I hope this discussion clarifies the sense in which God is complex and the different but important senses in which God is indeed simple.

I have argued that the hypothesis of God is fruitful, not in experimental science, but in philosophical thinking. It considerably raises the probability – to the point of virtual certainty – that the laws of nature should be as conducive to the emergence of intelligent life as they are. Nevertheless, the question remains: can the existence of God itself be explained? Only if it can will there be a truly final explanation for the universe.

3

Explaining God

Time for Turtles

Many people find it hard to understand how God can be the final explanation of everything. For, they say, when you have posited God as the explanation, you still have to face the question, 'Who made God?' That question is unanswerable. So your explanation has not really got you anywhere.

The point is made by Paul Davies in a little story that he sometimes tells of the woman who said that the universe rests on the back of a turtle. When asked, 'What does the turtle rest on?', she said, 'You can't get me there. It's turtles all the way down.'

So the question is, how can you put an end to the chain of turtles? Is God just one turtle among others, so that God must be explained by a super-God, who must be explained by a hyper-God, and so on without end?

There is, however, a totally convincing reply to the turtle objection. Forget God for a moment, and ask the question, 'Could there be a final explanation for why the universe is the way it is? If so, what would that explanation be like?'

Things in the universe exist in time. They come into being at a point in time, and we explain them, at least in science, by giving some initial state that is their cause, and some law of nature that things like that are always produced by causes like that.

Once we have given the cause and the law of nature, things are explained – we know why they are the sorts of things they are. So turtles are caused by other turtles, in accordance with laws of nature that tell us how mummy and daddy turtles produce baby turtles.

Everything that is in time is explained, it seems, by reference to a law and a preceding cause that brings it into being. But if we can think of something being in time, then it follows, by a simple process of negation, that we can also think of something not being in time. Call that an eternal thing. If there is an eternal thing, then it could not be brought into being by anything else, since it could not be brought into being at all. Since it is not in time, there never was a time when it was not, and it could not possibly be brought into being.

Perhaps an eternal thing could be dependent upon a more basic eternal thing, though that dependence would have to be eternal too. Presumably, however – and certainly, if there is to be a final explanation – there is at least one eternal thing that does not depend on anything else for its existence.

Such an eternal thing has no possible cause. It either is or it is not. But eternal things could be the cause of things in time, and indeed in modern physics time is often said to be caused by a super-temporal reality beyond it (for instance, by the vacuum state posited by some quantum theories).

Notice that a timeless cause is not the first thing in time. It is the cause of everything in time, whether time has a beginning and an end or not. From the timeless all times arise, and all things in time may depend upon the timeless – but they do not come after it.

Could there, then, be a timeless turtle that is the cause of all temporal turtles, but that cannot itself be caused or brought into being? The trouble with timeless turtles is that turtles seem, almost by definition, to be things that come into existence, grow and then die. So it is really hard to think of a timeless turtle. Even an immortal turtle, that lived forever, would not quite do, because it could in principle die at any time. What we need is a truly timeless turtle, which is not in time at all, and so could not possibly die, or be born either.

If we cannot quite think of a timeless turtle, perhaps we can at least think of a timeless cause of the whole pile of turtles. And that, really, is the first part of the answer to the question, 'Who made God?' The answer is that God is eternal, so nothing could possibly make God, cause God, bring God into being, or kill God either. Once you see that God is eternal, you will never again ask the question, 'Who or what made God?' You will see that the question does not make sense.

Necessary Turtles

You can, of course, still ask why God is the way God is, and how God explains the universe. To see how this question, too, can be answered quite successfully, we need to begin at the beginning again, and examine a little further what an explanation is.

We have seen that scientific explanations are usually given in terms of a cause and a law of nature. And we have seen that there could be an eternal cause, which is not itself capable of being caused. What needs explaining, in the case of the universe, is why the laws of nature are the way they are, when they could have been different in a huge number of ways.

An explanation of the universe is something that makes it more probable that the universe should be as it is. Ideally, the final explanation would make the universe virtually certain. But a truly final explanation would have to explain why the explanation itself is the way it is. It would have to be self-explanatory.

Can anyone think of such a thing? The best way to approach this question is to remember why the universe needs explaining in the first place. It needs explaining because it is contingent. The universe could have been different in millions of ways, or it might not have existed at all. It is precisely because there are so many alternative possibilities to the existence and nature of this universe that we want to explain why this particular possibility was realized.

We can at once see that the best explanation for the universe would be one that showed that in fact there are no alternatives; that the universe, just as it is, is necessary. If the universe has to be the way it is, if there are no alternative possibilities, that will be a final and completely satisfying explanation.

The trouble is that we can think of lots of alternative forms the universe could take. It is contingent. So if it has a final explanation, that must lie outside the universe, in some being that is necessary, to which there are no alternatives.

Can we think of something that could not fail to exist, that would be necessary? Modern cosmology suggests one possibility. Some cosmologists suggest that we live, not in a universe, one space-time, but in a multiverse, in which there are many space-times. Some argue that if you had a huge multiverse in which every possible combination of laws and constants was realized, then this universe would no longer be improbable. It would be certain – it is bound to exist somewhere in the multiverse.

Though it is very controversial, this hypothesis – the extreme multiverse hypothesis - would be a final explanation of the universe, since it would make the existence of our universe virtually certain. What it requires is that every possible universe exists. And that might be necessary – there might be no alternative to it. There are no other universes to think about, since all of them are in the set of 'all possible universes'. And that set has to be what it is, since if any universe is ever possible, then it is always possible, it always was possible and it always will be.

Possibilities, we might say, are eternal. They cannot come into being or pass away. They cannot be caused or brought about. If they are, they are, and if they are not, they are not. And that is that.

I suppose you could say that there might have been no possibilities at all. But in that case, nothing would ever exist, since there would be no possibility of anything existing. And if something is possible, then that possibility just is not the sort of thing that can come about, or that can be brought into being.

So the answer to the question, 'What made the set of all possible universes exist?', is that such a set is not the sort of thing that can be brought into being. It either always is or it never is. And, since there actually is something – because here we are – it obviously always is.

If you follow this train of thought, the turtle objection has already lost its main force. We can think of something that is not capable of being brought into being, that either always is or never could be. We have already made the distinction between the eternal (that which cannot be brought about) and the temporal (that which is in time, and so begins in time, and so needs a cause). Now we can make a distinction between the contingent (that which could be otherwise) and the necessary (to which there is no alternative). And we have seen that any final explanation for the universe will have to be both necessary and eternal, and so it cannot possibly be caused.

Of course, there are still questions for the multiverse, the set of all possible universes. Is there an actual infinite number of possible universes? If not, how many of them do we need to make this universe very probable? Can a 'set of all possibles' actually exist? And how do we know all of them are physically realized?

Probably the best answer to these questions, in physics, is that the set of all possibilities exists as a set of mathematical formulae (quantum laws) that are necessarily what they are. That set is physically realized by a random fluctuation of all balancing forces of inflation, gravity, electroweak and strong nuclear forces. This is often called 'quantum fluctuation in a vacuum'. It is a very full and active vacuum indeed, not just nothing! But if we could suppose that the quantum laws are somehow necessary, and that the process of fluctuation is also necessary, we have given a final explanation for the universe.

Exterminating Superfluous Turtles with Occam's Razor

What we have now is the set of all possible turtles, existing by necessity, and being physically realized, so that all possible turtles exist. It is turtles all the way down, after all. But, actually, hidden behind the turtles is a timeless and necessary set of turtle-possibilities, truly Platonic turtles. If that set exists, it would need no cause, and to it there would be no alternative – at least as far as turtles go. We have our final explanation of the universe, an explanation that can have no further explanation.

It has to be admitted, however, that this is a very extravagant theory. It completely contradicts the principle of Occam's Razor, which says that you should not multiply entities unnecessarily. One of Dawkins' main motivations is to explain the complex in terms of simpler parts and general laws. But that motivation disappears completely if we have an infinite number of universes, and every possible combination of laws. Dawkins resists this conclusion by saying that 'if each of those universes is simple in its fundamental laws, we are still not postulating anything highly improbable'.[1] That sounds like a desperate attempt to save a failed theory. The hypothesis that every possible universe exists is the most extravagant hypothesis anyone could think of, and it breaks Occam's rule of simplicity with a resounding smash. If the simple is good, then the fewer universes there are the better.

There are, Dawkins concedes, an extravagant number of universes. But they are all simple in their fundamental laws, and therefore not highly improbable. Unfortunately there is absolutely no reason to suppose that all universes are simple in their fundamental laws. Many of them, probably huge numbers of them, will have very complicated laws indeed. Even our universe does not seem as simple as Dawkins might like. And if 'extravagant numbers of universes' does not conflict with the theory of simplicity, it is hard to say what would.

I agree with Dawkins that it would be preferable to have a simpler, less extravagant theory, if we could. Luckily, such a theory exists. It is God. If you introduce God, you can say that all Platonic turtles do exist, but they all exist in the mind of God, who is not a turtle at all. The God hypothesis agrees completely with the argument that, if there is going to be a final explanation of the universe, it has to be in terms of an eternal and necessary being. But instead of having a huge set of complicated quantum laws and a very finely balanced set of fundamental physical forces, all of which are realized sooner or later by some unknown principle, it postulates just one being, a cosmic mind or consciousness.

The hypothesis of God is especially attractive, because it does not really look as though the fundamental laws and states of the universe are very simple at all. There is a whole 'particle zoo' at the subatomic level. There is dark energy and dark matter. There are many complex equations in quantum theory. The scientific search for one neat 'Theory of Everything', which would somehow embrace all lower-level physical laws, is looking very unlikely to succeed. The hypothesis that such a search will succeed is an article of faith in the power of science. It is not an unreasonable faith; there are good reasons, in the past success of science and the elegance of the laws so far discovered, to hold it. But to do so is as much a step of faith as is a commitment to the God hypothesis, which also has many good reasons to support it, but cannot at present be conclusively established.

Are the Laws of Nature Simple?

A significant problem in the philosophy of science arises at just this point. Are all the possibilities of the universe somehow already implicit in its primordial structure? In other words, are all the laws of nature present at the Big Bang, or do they change and develop with the developing universe? If all the laws always existed, then perhaps, if we knew all those laws in sufficient detail, we could predict, at least in general, all future possibilities – like, for instance, the emergence of intelligent life. On the other hand, there might be really new, emergent realities, not present at the first state of the universe, which might require new laws to correlate them with previous states of the cosmos.

The consciousness of animals might be one of those emergent realities. Could we know, for example, just from an examination of basic quantum laws and the basic forces of nature, that consciousness would result from the activity of very complex sets of neurons in the brains of animals? Our knowledge of Schrödinger equations, Hamiltonians, the cosmological constant and Planck's constant does not include any concept of consciousness. Consciousness seems to be an emergent property in our universe. It seems to emerge from very complex physical states, but it eludes description in purely physical terms.

Here is a possibility that could not be predicted from a knowledge of basic physical conditions. May there not be other possibilities, of which we know nothing? Of course, we could say that consciousness is just a supervenient property, one that is a by-product of physical forces, and is irrelevant to our calculations. Even then, the supervenient property could not be predicted from knowledge of basic quantum states alone. And if consciousness has causal consequences, as it seems to have, there will be emergent causes that would not be included in the original list of possible physical states.

What that means is that we could never be sure of knowing all the laws of nature (the constraints on possible states) until the story of the universe had unfolded. The law that consciousness will arise when a complex brain exists could not be known until after the event. Presumably the laws themselves exist as hypotheticals before the physical states exist. We can imagine them lying in wait (where?) for the right conditions to come about. But we can know them only when we see the causes and effects that exemplify those laws.

Since the universe has not yet finished developing, this means that we cannot in principle be sure of knowing all the laws of nature. But it looks very much as though the laws of nature cannot be reduced to a few simple and elementary principles that never require the addition of new principles.

Reductionists in the philosophy of science believe that all the laws of nature reduce to just a few basic laws, probably of physics. But, logically speaking, there may be laws that only apply to very complex states and the relations between them, which could not be predicted from, and are not entailed by, the simpler laws governing relations between elementary particles alone.

So it is not obvious, to say the least, that all the laws of nature reduce to a few simple laws. It looks more likely that there are many levels of laws, governing the relations between different kinds of entity at various levels of complexity and emergence.

Does this matter? Dawkins seems to think that the simpler a law is, the more probable it is. But is that so? I have shown that the term 'simple' has a number of different meanings, depending on the context in which it is used. When we talk about laws being simple, we are appealing to yet another sense of 'simple'.

What do we mean when we speak of a law of nature as simple? We certainly do not mean that laws are compounds, made up of simpler parts that are gradually added together.

We may mean that simple laws are elegant (not containing redundant parts), comprehensive (bringing many diverse phenomena under a few general principles), parsimonious (using as few variables as possible), and mathematically precise (with precisely ascertainable values).

Is it true that simple laws, in these senses, are more probable than complicated ones? I cannot see any reason at all for saying so. We may very much like to have laws that are elegant, comprehensive, parsimonious and mathematically precise. That will suit our aesthetic tastes. If the laws are like that, it will be a great and unexpected gift, as Eugene Wigner famously said.[2] But it is not by any means probable that the laws should be like that. If anything, it is amazingly improbable that the laws of nature should be so finely adjusted to our intellectual capacities.

The laws of this universe could easily have been different. The values of Planck's constant, the gravitational constant, the strong and weak nuclear forces, and the electromagnetic force could easily have been different. Physicists have shown that if they were, even by a minute degree, it is highly unlikely that carbon-based life-forms like us could ever have existed.

So we do have a probability problem about the laws of nature. The problem is not that the laws are complex. The problem is that they are only one set of possibilities among a whole range of alternatives, and it would be nice to have an explanation of why they are as they are. Such an explanation would have to raise the probability of the laws having the values they actually have, among all the values they could have had.

Is the Introduction of God Just Giving Up on Science?

Martin Rees, the Astronomer Royal, accepts that God is a possible final explanation for the universe. But he prefers the multiverse hypothesis.[3] I think the main reason for this is that the multiverse hypothesis looks like a properly scientific hypothesis, whereas the God hypothesis does not.

Once you introduce God, you have moved outside the realm of science. The mind of God may explain why this universe exists. But we have no public access to the mind of God, the hypothesis is not conclusively testable, and it gives rise to no specific predictions.

Dawkins puts this point in a very belligerent way. 'Religion', he says, 'teaches us that it is a virtue to be satisfied with not understanding.'[4] Introducing God into a theory is just a label for ignorance – 'If you don't understand how something works, never mind: just give up and say God did it.'[5]

I have to say that this is one of the most obviously false statements in the history of human thought. I fail to see how anyone who is concerned to get an accurate view of intellectual history, or of the history of science, could ever believe it, even for a moment. I cannot believe that Dawkins really believes it. He must, for his own rhetorical purposes, be manipulating or concealing the evidence.

Historically speaking, the Christian religion has very often functioned in exactly the opposite way. Isaac Newton was inspired to search for general laws of motion and mechanics precisely by the thought that the universe was designed by God, in which case its laws would be both intelligible and elegant. The scientific enterprise in its modern sense originated in a theistic culture, and most histories of science agree that belief in a God who created the universe through wisdom (in the Christian case, through *logos* or intellect) was a direct inspiration to scientific investigation into the causes of things.

Much religious thought teaches that the works of God can be understood by the minds of humans, who are created in the image of God. And this is a spur to further understanding, not a block to seeking the truth.

Yet even though Dawkins is demonstrably mistaken about what all religion teaches, and – astonishingly – about the history of science, I can see what he means. If you just say 'God did it' as an explanation, that may not stop further attempts to get other sorts of explanation, but it does not seem to provide a scientific explanation at all. There are no general laws revealed, no predictions possible, and no particular use that can be made of the explanation.

All this is true. God is not part of a scientific explanation. The reason is quite simple: God is part of a personal explanation, which is not reducible to scientific explanation, and has a different function. Personal explanations do explain why things happen as they do – broadly, because they are intended by some consciousness to realize some purpose which that consciousness finds desirable.

There are no general laws stating how personal beings will realize their purposes. We will not be able to predict exactly how they will act, and we will often not have access to their innermost desires and purposes. Nevertheless, personal explanations provide information. They tell us that there are purposes; they tell us in a general way what those purposes are likely to be; and they tell us that there is a mind-like reality, some apprehension of which may be possible or even likely. So the idea of God is not part of any scientific theory, and it does not block any sort of scientific search for understanding. It proposes to add a new dimension, the personal dimension, to understanding of the universe. It is therefore of great importance to take it seriously, if we are not to fall into the delusion that the personal dimension simply does not exist.

An Interlude on How Ideas of God Change and Develop

The God hypothesis proposes that there is an eternal and necessary mind that brings the universe into being for the sake of its distinctive goodness. This is information that may be extremely important. It will become important to discover, if we can, what the purpose of that mind is, what is really good about it, and what we may do to help realize it. It will become reasonable to think that the primordial mind may have communicated that purpose in some way, and so to look for plausible instances of such 'personal revelation' in history. All that may have a dramatic influence on our lives – an influence that Dawkins thinks would be almost wholly evil, which is possibly why he does not like the idea of a final personal explanation.

Whether Dawkins likes it or not, the idea is coherent. If he thinks that some alleged revelations of divine purpose are evil, then the reasonable course is to look for other revelations, or interpretations of revelation, that are good. That should not be difficult, since the most basic criterion of an authentic final personal explanation is that it aims at true goodness.

Many people may be mistaken about what true goodness is. Dawkins points out, quite rightly, that human moral perceptions have changed quite radically in recent years, from perceptions about slavery and human rights to perceptions about sexual equality and animal welfare. If our ideas of what is truly good change and (hopefully) develop, then obviously our ideas about what God, the primordial mind, aims at, will develop in corresponding ways.

At this point, Dawkins' sense of history seems to desert him. When he calls the God of the Old Testament 'a petty, unjust, unforgiving control-freak'[6] and worse, he is picking out moral perceptions from a Bronze Age set of documents that were actually in advance of most of the morally accepted beliefs of the time. This God was always the best sort of God – the ideal of moral perfection – that the people of the time could imagine.

The Old Testament records suggest that God inspired the minds of prophets and the biblical writers over quite a long period of time to move to new and deeper insights into what God demands and promises. But this was a gradual process that needed to accommodate itself to the history and culture of various times. For Jews, it culminated in the writings of the major prophets of the eighth to sixth centuries BC. For Christians, it culminated in the teachings of Jesus.

It would be ridiculous to talk about physics, and insist that Aristotle was to be accepted as the final authority in modern physics. Aristotle was a great scientist, and a hero of the intellectual life. But his opinions were necessarily limited in various ways by the knowledge available in the culture of ancient Greece.

It is equally ridiculous to talk about the biblical God, and insist that some Bronze Age reflections on what warfare requires, taken out of context, are to be accepted as the final authority on the morality of the biblical God. Such laws on war as are found in the book of Leviticus, for example, were formed in a vastly different period of history and technological development. Later prophetic reflection leads to a greatly modified view of what God really requires – 'I desire steadfast love and not sacrifice,' said the prophet Hosea (Hosea 6:6). And we can trace a development from the idea that God is 'a great King above all gods' (Psalm 95:3), to the statement that there is only one God, and there are no others (Isaiah 45:14).

What Dawkins fails to point out is that early biblical texts cannot be read in isolation from the totality of the Bible. What the Bible offers is a history of the development of the idea of God in ancient Hebrew religion. As such, it is a precious document of religious history, and one reason why it is important to read it now is precisely to see how religious ideas developed over thousands of years in one Middle Eastern tribal tradition.

That tradition reached one new plateau of religious understanding at the time of the major prophets, between the sixth and eighth centuries BC. It was then that the idea of one God of justice and mercy for all people definitively emerged. Remarkably, Dawkins never quotes from Isaiah or Amos, whose writings both criticize and amend earlier beliefs in vindictive punishment and tribal chauvinism.

Even then, the development of religious insight was not straightforward. For Christians, the teaching of Jesus puts the whole biblical teaching in a new light, making it quite clear that God's love is unlimited, and God's mercy and forgiveness are infinite. This, for Christians, is a fulfilment of the prophetic tradition, but it is one that gives a dramatically new perspective on the idea of God. And the process of interpretation continues, largely by reflection on the sorts of moral purposes that the universal and supremely good creator revealed in Jesus would have, and on different ways of applying these insights to new and sometimes rapidly changing circumstances.

This has been a sort of intermission in the argument, to explain why the 'God of the Old Testament', as described by Dawkins, is a biased selection of negative texts from early in a long biblical tradition, a tradition which contains vitally important qualifications and supplementations of those texts. But it also explains some of Dawkins' hostility to religion, which is basically hostility to those forms of religious belief which overlook or deny that such a process of development and interpretation ever took place. There are such forms of religion. I agree with Dawkins that they can be irritating and sometimes harmful. But I disagree with Dawkins that they are the only, or the 'proper', forms of religion.

Nevertheless, all this shows that the introduction of a final personal explanation of the universe has a close connection with revelation and thus with religion. That could be one reason why

Martin Rees is wary of mixing up such explanations with science, the practice of which has no direct connection with religion.

As I have shown, appealing to a final personal explanation is not giving up on the attempt to find scientific explanations for as many things as possible. It is not saying, 'There is a personal God who just wants things to be this way; so you may as well give up trying to understand it.' Scientific explanation should be pushed as far as it can go. Belief in God supports this push, because it guarantees that the universe is ultimately intelligible. But it adds that scientific explanation is not the only form of explanation. Scientific explanation drives you back, in the end, to eternity and necessity – to the realm of timeless and necessary mathematical truths, to ultimately intelligible laws and fundamental forces. But what is also needed for a final explanation is appeal to consciousness, value, creativity and purpose. Personal explanation complements, but does not replace, scientific explanation. Both are necessary to a truly final explanation of the universe.

4

God and the Multiverse

Three Multiverse Theories

It is because Martin Rees sees God and the multiverse as competing explanations that he expresses, as a committed scientist, a preference for the multiverse, despite its enormous ontological extravagance. There is no need to see this as a competition. God and the multiverse can easily co-exist. I will go further, and suggest that they do co-exist, that the hypothesis of the multiverse without God has numerous internal problems that God can readily resolve. But God does not do so as another scientific hypothesis. God is a fundamental metaphysical hypothesis about the ultimate nature of reality, and God leaves the investigations of science fully intact.

What, then, are the problems of the multiverse?[1] One complication is that there are many different sorts of multiverses. Dawkins mentions three, and I shall add two others. The first is the Hugh Everett 'many-worlds' interpretation of quantum mechanics. Though it is an important and interesting theory, I shall regard this as irrelevant to the question of why the laws of nature are as they are. This is because the many-worlds interpretation assumes that the laws and constants of nature remain the same in all the parallel worlds of quantum theory. So it does not answer our cosmological question. It only complicates life for quantum physicists.

The second theory, one mentioned by Dawkins, is the hypothesis that each universe expands and then collapses again into the 'Big Crunch'. Then a slightly different universe expands, with a slightly different set of laws and constants. As he says, this serial multiverse view is not favoured by contemporary cosmology, which sees this universe as irreversibly expanding until it finally runs out of energy.

The third theory is the Lee Smolin hypothesis that baby universes are born in black holes by a sort of random mutation process.[2] Those that survive produce more black holes and more babies, and so mutated universes are produced by a hyper-Darwinian cosmic algorithm. Sooner or later one of these babies will produce intelligent life, and this is the one.

This hypothesis requires that there is a set of super-laws that lays out the conditions of cosmic replication and mutation. So it does not resolve the problem of why the super-laws are as they are. Maybe that problem has no solution. But in that case, resorting to a multiverse does not help to solve the problem of why the laws of our universe are as they are. It would be more parsimonious (simpler) just to have the laws of our universe as brute facts, when the physics of baby universes in black holes is so very speculative and probably untestable. In any case, it is not directly relevant to the quest for a final explanation, since the explanation it provides is not final.

The Inflationary Hypothesis

A fourth multiverse hypothesis, also mentioned by Dawkins, is sometimes called the 'inflationary' hypothesis. Each universe is like a bubble; many bubbles are spread out in space and possibly in time; and all universes together form a bubbly multiverse, with different sets of laws in each universe. If the multiverse is big enough, our universe may well be produced by chance through some natural process. It helps to raise the probability of our universe existing if it is one of many universes that take different values, and that exist by some sort of necessity.

It is far from clear whether this hypothesis does raise the probability of our universe existing. How many different universes are there, and why do they exist as they do? This, too, is not a final explanation, since the super-laws governing the multiverse still need explaining.

You might say, however, that the laws of our universe are contingent, for they could easily have been otherwise. But the laws of the multiverse may be necessary. They may be sets of mathematically possible universes, perhaps all the universes that could physically exist. Now you have the desired appeal to necessity, which attracts even Dawkins. 'It is indeed perfectly plausible that there is only one way for a universe to be,' he says.[3] It does not seem plausible to say that the laws of our universe are strictly necessary, since they could have been otherwise. But maybe there is a deeper set of super-laws which, being mathematically exhaustive and complete, covering all possibilities, could be truly necessary.

A mathematically exhaustive theory would set out the exhaustive array of all possible states. This is a sort of neo-Platonic hypothesis, to which Roger Penrose, among others, is inclined. The world of sense-perceptions, the three-dimensional world of flowing time, is an appearance of a deeper mathematical reality of Hamiltonians and Hilbert spaces and imaginary time, which is eternal and changeless, and underlies every possible physical universe.

This, it seems, would at last fulfil the dream of a final theory. The answer to the question 'Why are the laws as they are?' is 'This set of possibilities is exhaustive and all-inclusive. There is no alternative to it. There is only one way for it to be. It cannot be brought into being or pass away. It has to be what it is; it is mathematically necessary.'

I am impressed that Dawkins shares that dream, at least sometimes. It is the dream of philosophically-minded theists too. For a theist, the exhaustive set of mathematical possibilities describing every possible universe and state of affairs does exist. It exists in the mind of God. The reference to God is not a superfluous addition. It has explanatory advantages.

One advantage of existence in the mind of God is that the mind of God is an eternal and necessary actual being. Mathematical possibilities seem to be precisely that – possibilities – and it seems plausible to suppose that there must be something actual in which possibilities exist. Casting around for analogies, the obvious one is that possible states of affairs exist as conceived in minds. So the best place for mathematical possibilities to exist is in a cosmic mind or intelligence – a view that Roger Penrose seems to sympathize with.

A second advantage of existence in the mind of God is that God, being necessarily actual, and thus having the power of existence in the divine being, will be able to make possibilities actual. There will also be a simple principle of their actualization. God will make universes actual for the sake of envisaged goodness.

That is why the multiverse is not an alternative to God. The hypothesis of God actually makes the multiverse hypothesis, in some sense (the sense in which all universes exist in the mind of God), more intelligible. It also positively adds elements to explanation that a purely physical hypothesis does not. For the hypothesis of an ultimate creative consciousness explains the existence of finite consciousness, of creativity, and of purpose and value, in a universe that is not solely physical in nature.

Breathing Fire into the Equations

Take away God, and personal explanation disappears. What also disappears is a very good reason for the existence of a universe containing intelligent, finite minds. We are left with the question that Stephen Hawking asked in *A Brief History of Time*: 'What is it that breathes fire into the equations and makes a universe for them to describe?'[4]

The world of necessity, of exhaustive possibility, does not seem to entail the existence of any physically existent and actual universe. You could just say, like Spinoza, that all possibilities are actualized. But if it is highly improbable that a particular one out of the set of possible universes should exist, then it is even more improbable that two specific universes should exist. It might seem that the more universes there are, the less probable the whole thing is, and the existence of every possible universe is hugely more improbable than the existence of just one improbable universe. But the calculation gets difficult when we do not know exactly how many possible universes there are, and impossible if it should happen to be an infinite number.

Perhaps what we should say is that we do not know how to calculate the probability of any universes existing, since the coming into being of a universe is not just like a standard case of probability theory – for example, measuring the probability of picking a red ball out of a bag of many-coloured balls, when it is known how many balls there are and what colours they are. You might say that if you keep pulling single balls out of a bag of a thousand balls, then sooner or later you will pull a specific coloured ball out of the bag. But the coming into existence of universes is not like that. For there is nothing that exists to begin with – just possibilities of existing. There is no analogy to pulling balls out of a bag when you are only considering possible balls – you do not know how many or of what nature – in possible bags. But that is what you are trying to do when thinking of the origin of universes.

Thus if you ask what the probability is that all possible worlds will exist, there is no sensible answer. It is like asking what the probability is that someone will pull all the balls out of the bag at the same time. You are changing the rules of probability out of all recognition.

The multiverse hypothesis does not require that all possible universes exist. It just says that a lot of universes exist – some proponents of M theory suggest that there are 10 to the power of 500 universes, but that is a bit of a shot in the dark. Physicists such as George Ellis doubt whether such theories are really scientific any more, since it is hard to see what predictions they produce.[5] They are at least sixteen orders of magnitude beyond possible observation. And they seem to require laws with very precise values for the symmetry-breaking that will produce the right sort of vacuum energy and balance of inflation and gravity to form a universe.

The existence of a huge number of universes, all with differing fundamental forces and constants, would increase the probability that this universe would exist. That is probably the main attraction of string theory in cosmology. But something must cause the forces and constants to vary in a systematic way in order to cover the whole range of different possibilities. And something must cause the multiverse to exist, since it too seems to be ultimately contingent.

The cosmological search has, in the end, just been put back a stage, so that we now have to ask: what accounts for the hyper-laws of the multiverse? I can imagine Dawkins protesting that God is in just the same situation. But that is not true. God, being necessary and eternal, does not require the same sort of explanation that is required for contingent and temporal universes. However, there might be something that is necessary and eternal, but is not God, which might be more acceptable to hard-headed physicists.

Problems of the Extreme Multiverse

This leads back to talk of an exhaustive and necessary set of possible universes. This is a fifth sort of multiverse, one advocated by Max Tegmark, in which every mathematically possible universe actually exists.[6] Yet the paradoxes and problems of such a multiverse seem to me insuperable. Let me just mention a few.

First, there is a problem about what sorts of universes are possible. Tegmark is thinking about purely physical values for the forces and constants of a universe, but I would have thought that among possible universes is one with God as its creator. Why could we not exist in that one? Indeed, as the American philosopher Alvin Plantinga has argued, if there is a possible universe in which God exists as a necessary being, and if 'necessary' means 'actual in all possible universes', then if God exists in any actual universe, there will be no possible universe without God.[7]

This is not the infamous Ontological Argument, which some take to prove that God exists simply by an analysis of some concepts in human minds. Rather, it is saying that if God ever actually exists, then God always and everywhere exists, because that is what God is. To put it another way, if God really is the one necessarily existing and eternal cause of all contingent and temporal beings, then no world without God is even possible – even though such worlds may seem possible to us.

This argument is analytical. It does not prove that God exists. It carefully analyses the idea of God (as Dawkins does not), and draws the conclusion that if the idea is coherent, and if God exists, then there is no possible universe that could exist without God. Atheism, if it is false, is necessarily false (there is no possible world without God). It is the extreme multiverse hypothesis that leads to the necessary falsity of atheism. That is probably a reason for Dawkins not to accept it.

There are other features of the extreme multiverse hypothesis that Dawkins would not like. If every possible state is realized somewhere, a virgin birth is bound to happen sooner or later. Indeed, if every possible physical state and combination of states will exist sooner or later, then in some universe there are miracles of every possible sort continually taking place, and that universe could be ours!

For Dawkins, however, as for his eminent philosophical predecessor David Hume, what would seem to be a very improbable physical possibility is ruled out by the laws of nature. That means a decisive rejection of the proposal that everything that is possible is bound to happen sooner or later.

I have to say that once more I agree with Dawkins in my dislike of the extreme multiverse hypothesis. For virgin births and resurrections are not, like God, necessary. So while virgin births and resurrections will happen in some universes, they will not happen in others. The Christian faith will be true in some universes, and not in others. Every religion, however weird, as long as it is not self-contradictory, will be true in some universe. This proposal will, I think, annoy both Dawkins and me to an equal degree (though on second thoughts I doubt that I could ever get quite as annoyed as Dawkins does).

To generalize this point, if every possible universe exists, then there must be quite a lot of universes in which the laws of nature do not operate at all, or in which they stop operating at some arbitrary time. Since we are not quite sure which universe we are in, we would never be able to rely on the constancy of the laws of nature, and we could never justifiably trust that the future will be like the past. The principle of induction would fail.

The fact that we do not believe this shows that we do not take the extreme multiverse seriously. We think the laws of nature will continue to be reliable. This entails a strong faith or commitment, well beyond the evidence, to the rule of law in nature. The extreme multiverse hypothesis undermines such commitment. The God hypothesis strongly supports it, by the simple consideration that a rational God will ensure that nature is reliable enough to make human understanding, prediction and manipulation of the universe possible and profitable.

Another strange feature of the extreme multiverse hypothesis is that it entails that all universes, however evil and horrific they are, will exist. We may think that God has not done a very good job with this universe. But at least it is much better than some of the universes that exist in the extreme multiverse, which are utterly and irredeemably evil.

Tegmark has argued further that, in an infinite array of universes, everything will not only happen, everything will happen an infinite number of times. Not only will I kill and eat my mother in some universe, I will do it over and over again. That thought is unbearable enough to make God morally necessary. The least a good God can do is to prevent the extreme multiverse, with lots of copies of me in it, all doing terrible things over and over again, from existing.

Why God Beats the Multiverse

I conclude that the extreme multiverse is a non-starter. Its claimed advantage is that it makes this universe highly probable, by supposing that every possible universe is bound to exist. But it is hugely improbable that all universes should exist. The addition of a huge number of improbabilities does not, after all, add up to one certainty. It is true that, if all possible universes exist, then this universe will exist. But it is not true that it is more probable that all possible universes exist than that one or two of them should exist, or that none of them should. Quite the reverse. The physical existence of all possible universes is just one possibility among many others (that one of them should exist, that two of them should, and so on…). So the multiverse hypothesis may increase the probability of this universe existing. But it does not remove the huge improbability of all possible universes existing!

Luckily we can retain the advantages of the multiverse hypothesis, while dispensing with its huge disadvantages, in a very simple way. We can say that all possible universes do indeed necessarily exist. But they exist as possibilities in the mind of God. God will only actualize those of them (one or more, we do not know) that meet the criterion of having great and distinctive goodness.

The multiverse hypothesis at first looks promising as an alternative to God. But it depends on making two insupportable assumptions. The first is that a specific probability can be assigned to every possible state of affairs, and thus that every possible state of affairs can be known and specified. Only if we could do that could we assign an exact probability to the existence of a particular universe, whether complex or simple. Only then could we compare the probability of God to the probability of a simple universe, or a complex universe, or the actual existence of all possible universes.

But we would then have to know all possible combinations of laws and constants. Unfortunately, we have not the slightest idea of what that would be, or how many different sorts of basic forces and laws there might be in other universes. There is no way of calculating such probabilities. So we cannot say – in the abstract, and without any constraints posed by an existing universe – what the probability of any state existing, whether simple or complex, is.

The second assumption is that every possible state will occur, given enough time. That is what makes it certain that this universe will occur, given enough time. But is this true?

We have seen that the postulate that every possible state will exist has totally unacceptable consequences, and is supremely undesirable. We have also seen that the postulate is in any case untrue if there are any laws that govern the coming into being of possible states. Such laws will entail, or perhaps make probable, some states, and rule out the existence of others. Without knowing whether there are any such laws for a multiverse, or what they are, we are in no position to say what or how many possible states may become actual.

The God hypothesis avoids these implausible assumptions by refraining from stating that each universe has a finite probability of existing, and that everything with a finite probability will exist sooner or later. On the God hypothesis, no universe has any probability of existing unless God chooses to create it, and God's choice prevents many evil universes from existing. We may say that good universes are more probable than evil ones, but that probability rests on acceptance of a fundamental personal explanation, and is not part of a scientific explanation at all.

I conclude that the multiverse hypothesis, while it is an interesting attempt to render the laws of this universe more probable, ultimately fails as a final explanation. Such an explanation requires an appeal to necessity, and the eternal and necessary existence of all possible universes might provide that. But there is no path from possibility to actual existence by way of scientific explanation, except the path of postulating the necessary physical existence of all possible universes. While that cannot be absolutely ruled out, it entails great disadvantages that can be avoided by introducing personal explanation and the existence of possible universes in the mind of a God who has the capacity to create universes for the sake of their goodness. For the mind of God combines eternal and necessary existence with consciousness of and desire for goodness. Thus the God hypothesis is both more parsimonious and more comprehensive than the extreme multiverse hypothesis. As such, it is rational to prefer it.

Turtles Again

It is vitally important that we do not think of God as some sort of human-like being with lots of fairly arbitrary characteristics. That idea has never been supported by a leading theologian of any major monotheistic tradition. God is the mind in which all possible universes and states of being exist. Since that set of possible states is necessary (there is no alternative possibility that is not already in it), the mind of God is also necessary. Since the set of possible states is timeless, the mind of God is also timeless.

The God hypothesis makes the idea of an exhaustive set of possible universes more intelligible. For if we just think of possible states, we might well ask how the merely possible can actually exist. Existing in an actual mind gives them somewhere to be, and that seems to make good sense, when we remember that in ordinary experience possible states are conceived by minds. The merely possible cannot really exist, unless it exists in something actual. A mind is the most obvious place in which to put possible turtles (ideas of turtles that may or may not exist).

Moreover, introducing a timeless and necessary mind gives a good explanation of why some possible states should become physically actual. On the extreme multiverse hypothesis, all possible states become actual. But it is hard to see why this should be so. It would be good to have a reason why they should all exist, or why only some of them, even perhaps only one of them, should exist.

If possible states exist in a mind, we can at once provide a reason – and the best possible reason – why some or all possible states should exist. Quite simply, it is because that mind finds their actual existence to be intrinsically desirable, worthwhile and enjoyable.

This obvious and natural thought points to the fact that the discussion of possible universes in physics usually proceeds (as things usually do in cosmology) as though all possible universes were purely physical. When you have stated the physical conditions and physical laws of a universe, you have said everything there is to be said about a universe.

But that omits the most important thing about our universe – the existence in it of many forms of consciousness. Perhaps it is assumed that consciousness is just a by-product of material processes, and that it has no causal part to play in any universe. That assumption may be widespread among physicists, but it plainly contradicts common sense experience.

I normally suppose that I am conscious of the world, and that I can decide to do things in it. I frame purposes, aiming at states I think to be of value, and I cause various acts to come about that may produce those states. My purposes are states that I think to be of value, and value is, most basically, whatever I desire and enjoy. Thus, as argued in the first chapter, personal explanation has to be somehow included in any comprehensive account of the way the world is.

I propose that consciousness, though in the human case it is a factor that emerges from the physical development of the brain, is an irreducible fact, like energy or matter. A conscious state is not just a physical state. It has its own proper reality, and no account of reality that ignores it can be complete.

If that is so, the ultimate constituents of the universe, out of which the whole complex universe is made, cannot just be lumps of matter or fields of force. They must include conscious states. Though animal conscious states – including the human – emerge from complex brains, they are truly emergent, new sorts of reality, and they stand in need of an explanation that cannot be reduced to physical terms alone.

It is hard to imagine that there could be conscious states within the universe before brains evolve, so such states would have to exist outside our space-time, or as some sort of potential-for-consciousness, to be realized when physical conditions have become complex enough.

The Priority of Mind

The natural way to think of this, and the way that has been taken by the vast majority of classical philosophers, is to posit the simplest or most economical form of consciousness – namely, just one conscious mind that shapes or brings about the physical universe in order to actualize many emergent conscious states through a long, gradual process of development.

However conscious states come about, once they exist they require not just scientific explanation, but personal explanation. The God hypothesis, at its simplest, is the hypothesis that personal explanation is not reducible to scientific explanation, and that it is prior to scientific explanation. That is, the causal states and laws described by scientific explanation are ultimately to be explained in terms of the reasons that a thinking and feeling and acting mind could have for choosing them. They are chosen because they are, to some consciousness, of intrinsic desirability or goodness.

Put another way, mind is prior to matter. Mind causes matter to exist, as a means of bringing into being a set of states that are desired and enjoyed by that mind, or that can be desired and enjoyed by other minds that may form a shared community.

The God hypothesis proposes that there is a consciousness that does not depend on any material brain, or on any material thing at all. In this consciousness all possible worlds exist, though only as possible states that may or may not actually exist. The cosmic consciousness can evaluate these possible worlds in terms of their desirability – their beauty or elegance or fecundity, for example. Then, being actual, it can bring about desirable states and enjoy them.

God can, in other words, think of all possible turtles, can discern that many of them are interesting and beautiful, can decide to make some of them exist precisely because of that discernment, and then can just enjoy them for what they are. This provides an excellent reason for the existence of turtles – God enjoys them. And there is also an excellent reason for the existence of God – God has to exist if any turtles are to be possible at all (if there is to be a set of all possible turtles). All Platonic turtles necessarily exist in the mind of God, who will create some possible turtles for the sake of the value they have, because they are interesting and beautiful.

I think, therefore, that God is the best final explanation there can be for the universe. Indeed, if there is a final explanation for the universe, it virtually has to be God! The probability of this universe having the laws and constants it does is raised, as cosmologists generally say it is, by appeal to the exhaustive array of possible worlds that exist by necessity. But we can avoid the needless extravagance of saying that all these worlds actually exist by positing that they all exist in the mind of God, which is just one simple entity, not being composed of separable parts.

Then we can account for the actual existence of this universe by appeal to just one simple principle – it exists for the sake of its distinctive goodness, and is selected by God for that reason. All the laws and constants of our universe exist because they make possible the distinctive sorts of goodness our universe contains. And God has chosen those sorts of goodness as intrinsically worthwhile.

The final explanation of our universe is the eternal and necessary mind of God. This is not a proof of God that would convince even a materialist. Yet it shows something important that Dawkins denies. It shows that if there *is* a final explanation – and many scientists think there should or must be – then God is it. That means that if the universe is rational, God almost certainly exists.

Far from belief in God being some sort of irrational leap of faith, it is the most rational hypothesis there is; and perhaps it is the only plausible and sure foundation of the rationality of the universe that science presupposes.

5

Objections and Replies

Can Pure Consciousness Exist?

My argument against the Boeing 747 gambit is almost complete. But there are some questions the argument needs to face before it can be accepted as truly satisfactory.

The first question is whether a pure consciousness, without any material context or basis, can exist. I confess that I cannot see much force in the statement that a pure consciousness is impossible. There is no contradiction in the idea. We can think of being aware of trees, people, thoughts and feelings without having a physical body. I agree that does not prove that minds can exist without bodies in fact, but it does mean the onus is on those who think it is impossible, to prove it.

The mind of God would not be like any human mind. Human minds are dependent on brains, on a physical environment, and on being given information. A divine mind would be totally independent. Its information would not come from outside, but would be part of its own being. Human minds depend on many external and contingent factors for their knowledge, and act on many different and often irrational principles. But in God, the knowing subject and the things known are parts of the same being, and do not depend upon anything external. The things known (in the first place, all possible states) are necessarily what they are.

Divine knowledge would not be contingent, so we would not have to explain why the information it contains is as it is. A divine mind is simple in the second sense defined earlier – it does not depend on many contingent and separate things, all of which might be otherwise. Its mental content is necessary and self-generated. That content has one source – itself – and it has to be the way it is.

Moreover, the divine mind acts on one simple and wholly rational principle – for the sake of goodness. In all these ways, while the content of the divine mind is very complex, that mind is simple in a number of senses that human or finite minds cannot possibly share.

So Dawkins is quite wrong when he argues that God would have to be more complex, and therefore more improbable, than any universe that God creates. A physical universe is complex in that it is composed of many contingent parts, which could easily have been otherwise, that fall into complex integrated patterns without any prior plan or purpose. But God is not composed of parts; the being of God is necessary, not contingent; God is one being that is the source of all that exists; and there is one very good reason why God and the universe exist – because it is good that they should. In all these ways, God is not more complex than the universe. And God is not improbable, since God is either impossible or necessary, but not somewhere in between.

God is not just a projection of a humanoid mind onto the external world. Philosophically speaking, we frame the idea of God by asking what the simplest and most self-explanatory idea of mind would be. The idea is the result of abstract reflection on the nature of reality, and it is radically unlike the starting-point of reflection, the conscious states of human beings.

When we start thinking about the ultimate nature of matter, of course we start from things like trees and rocks and bodies. But we soon move into a very different area, of quarks and electrons. So it is with God. We start with human conscious states. But we move into the very different area of a necessary consciousness of all possible states, and action on one purely rational principle. That is pushing the idea of mind to its limit, and it is not at all like projecting human thoughts onto physical things.

Sometimes people ask, 'How can such a pure mind, even if it is possible, cause matter to exist?' But the proper answer to that question is to ask how anything, physical or otherwise, can cause – bring into existence – anything else at all! We simply do not know how anything can cause anything else. For a mental state to produce a physical state does not seem to be any more difficult than for one physical state to produce another, or for a physical state to produce a mental state. All causal relations are a mystery to us.

But I do think there is force in the classical philosophical axiom that, for a truly explanatory cause to be intelligible, it must in some way contain its effects potentially in itself. As the classical philosophers put it, the cause must contain more reality than its effects. The whole universe, in its most complex possible forms, must somehow be contained potentially in its cause.

If you feel this has force, it is another reason for postulating that the cause of the universe is a being that contains the potentialities of all things – that knows what those potentialities are, and has the power to actualize them. Maybe this is just a very basic difference of perception, one of those basic ontological choices in philosophical thinking. Either things are all in the end material, and develop without purpose from some simple initial material state. Or the ultimate reality is mind, a perfect mind containing all possible things within itself in a different manner, and causing some of them to exist physically in order to realize some purpose – perhaps the purpose of creating other minds to share in the good things it enjoys. In making such a basic ontological choice, close attention will have to be paid to all aspects of human knowledge and experience. If this is done, the materialist hypothesis may begin to lose its initial attraction.

Can the Necessary Produce the Contingent?

This talk of potentialities raises another important issue. Even if God, a purely spiritual being, can cause a physical universe to exist, still, if God is necessary and timeless, how can such a being produce a contingent and temporal universe?

The problem is this: if God is necessary, then God cannot do other than God does. But if the universe is contingent, then the universe could have been other than it is. Now if God creates the universe, and has to do what God does, it seems that the universe has to be what it is. There is no alternative to it. Both Spinoza and Leibniz agreed about this, though they did not agree about how many universes God would create (Spinoza thought lots, Leibniz thought God would only create the best one).

To put that point the other way around, if the universe is really contingent, and God creates it, then there must be something contingent about God after all – the divine act of creating a contingent universe must itself be contingent. Are we stuck with a contradiction?

We are not. But we do need to say that God is both necessary and contingent: necessary in some respects and contingent in others. God is necessary in existence and in knowing all possible states, and in having the ability to actualize any possible state. But God is contingent in the choice of which states to actualize, and in any subsequent divine interactions with those states.

This is an important refinement to the idea of God, which was first clearly made by philosophers such as Hegel in the nineteenth century. We have seen that if God is to be a final explanation, God must be both necessary and timeless. But that does not mean that God cannot also be contingent and temporal in some ways. In fact it could be a necessary part of God's nature (something that God could not exist without) to be able to make free, creative and therefore contingent choices.

God is not limited by timelessness and necessity. There must be something timeless and necessary about God – basically, the divine existence as creative mind and the set of all possible states in the divine mind. But there might also be a place – even a necessary place – for creative choice.

To make this clear, it may help if we think of a hypothetical human person who has to exist and who is necessarily good. She cannot do evil or commit suicide or die, even if she wants to. There are no actual humans like that, but there could be. That person, however, might still have lots of choices about what particular good things to do, and about where and how she is going to exist. She might, for instance, just have to love people. But she might have some choice about whom to love, or in what way exactly to express her love.

It is the same with God, though of course God's choices will never be fickle or arbitrary in a way that a human person's choices might be. God necessarily exists, knows all possibles, and is a creative mind. But within those boundaries, God is free to be creative in many different ways. Since that could be an essential part of God's nature, there is no real problem with the idea at all. What it does is clarify the point that God is not locked into a permanently frozen, changeless immobility. God is always free to act and respond creatively. But God will always and necessarily act for good.

Such creative choice is not without a cause. The cause is a choosing mind. And it is not without a reason. The reason is to bring new sorts of good things or states into being. But there is no *determining* cause or reason – one to which there are no alternatives. There is a realm of freedom in God. And since such freedom is a necessary condition of personal explanation (free choice for the sake of good), it must exist if God is to be the final personal explanation for the universe.

Once more, the important point is that creativity and mind, value and purpose, have to be included in any final explanation of the universe. Materialism is deficient as a philosophy because it cannot include them, and has to argue them out of existence. If they are to be included, the simplest way to do so is to postulate one mind, necessary in existence and free in creative action, which is the cause of the complex physical universe, for the sake of bringing into being many different sorts of goods that may be enjoyed in many different ways by many different finite minds.

Are There Objective and Universal Goods?

For some people it makes no sense to speak of 'goods' or values, as though there was one set of values that all could agree upon. All values, they say, are just what people happen to like, and values vary enormously from person to person. So there is no set of values that God would be bound to choose.

God, however, cannot just 'happen to like' various things or states. God necessarily knows all possible states. Does God thereby know that some are 'better' or more valuable than others, and perhaps that some are of no value at all?

I think that the answer to this question is plainly 'yes'. If God envisages being in agonizing pain (supposing that is possible for God), then this is a bad and undesirable state. But if God envisages being intensely happy, that is good and desirable. There is no question at all that happiness is more desirable than pain. So God will know that happiness is better, more valuable, than pain.

Objections to this very obvious point usually consist in saying that someone might choose pain for the sake of some other good. No rational person thinks that anyone would choose pain that leads to no other good, just for its own sake. Happiness is intrinsically good; a rational being would choose it for its own sake, as long as it did not lead to later harm or evil. So there is at least one intrinsic good.

There are many other intrinsic goods. Among them, knowledge, power and creativity (in the sense of ability to do things) are intrinsic goods that every rational being has reason to choose for their own sake. It is thus natural that God would choose the highest possible happiness, knowledge and power, and that the divine being would actualize in itself the highest possible degree of intrinsic goodness. And that is what it means to say that God is supremely good.

In fact, the classical Western definition of God, formulated by Anselm, Archbishop of Canterbury, in his statement that God is 'that than which nothing greater (more perfect) can be conceived', states exactly that.[1] This formula, incidentally, gives another sense in which the being of God is 'simple'. God can be defined in a unique and very concise way, and Anselm did it in his definition.

It has since become clear that, as we proceed to work out in more detail what the supremely good being would involve, disagreements can arise. Perhaps the main one is that Anselm thought that a perfectly good God would have to be wholly changeless, because any change would be for the worse. But since Hegel many philosophers have thought that a God who could not change at all would not be the most perfect possible being. Rather, they argue, being able creatively to bring new sorts of value into existence is a positive good. And that entails the possibility of change in God – not change either for the better or for the worse, but just change that expresses the creative power of God in ever-new ways.

Many philosophers also think that relationship, or the sharing of love, experience and activity, is a positively good thing. So a perfectly good being would either have to include relationship within the divine being (thus the Christian doctrine of the Trinity), or God would have to create other minds with which relationships could take place.

These disagreements show that it is not easy to say exactly what a supremely good being will be like, and there can be genuine differences of opinion about it. But virtually all believers in God will agree that God is supremely good. This shows how thought about God requires reflection and argument, and is not just a matter of blind faith. It also shows how ideas of God develop in accordance with changes in moral and factual beliefs. They do not stay the same forever, but need to be continually rethought.

These considerations provide a reason for the existence of a universe. The creation of a universe gives scope for divine creativity; it enables God to appreciate and enjoy many actually existing things, as well as just contemplating their possibility; it makes possible a relationship of the divine mind to finite minds; and it brings into being new minds that can enjoy value in new ways.

Why Does Evil Exist?

These are all good reasons for creating a universe. But, if these are God's reasons, why is our universe not much better than it seems to be? Voltaire made great fun of Leibniz's belief that God, being good, must have created the best of all possible worlds. Surely this universe, with all the waste and frustration and pain in it, could not be the best possible world?

The Leibniz proposal is not as ridiculous as it may seem, however. Perhaps all the better universes we think we can imagine are not really possible. American physicist Steven Weinberg suggests that there may be only one consistent mathematical theory, one 'logically isolated' theory, that can produce intelligent life.[2] And the basic laws of nature are such that they are bound to produce destructive as well as creative forces. Some suffering is therefore necessary in a life-producing universe.

Much the same thought occurred to Einstein, who wrote, 'The aim of physics is not only to know how nature is and how her transactions are carried through, but also to reach as far as possible the utopian and seemingly arrogant aim of knowing why nature is thus and not otherwise... that God himself could not have arranged these connections in any other way.'[3] If you could show that the universe is necessary, and that its existence is the condition of great and not otherwise obtainable goods, even that it is the only one that can support intelligent life, Leibniz might be right after all!

If Weinberg is right, and there is only one set of laws and constants that can produce intelligent beings like us, then in imagining that we, or beings very like us, could exist in a very different universe, we are just wrong.

It is very difficult to establish that this really is the only universe that could support any form of intelligent life. What we might say, however, is that it is the only universe that can support intelligent life *like us*.

If we are to exist, maybe we just have to be in this universe. Perhaps there could be beings better than us, existing in a universe better than ours. But we would not be there (some of us hope, by divine help, to become fitted for such a better universe after we have finished existing in this one. It used to be called 'heaven' or Paradise – but that is another story).

Thus we might amend Leibniz's account a little. We could say, not that this is the best of all possible worlds, but that it is the only possible world that would allow us, and the distinctive sorts of values and good things that we can enjoy, to exist. It might, in other words, be a good reason for the existence of this universe that it realizes distinctive sorts of values that could not exist in any other universe.

Thomas Aquinas, who did not accept that there was just one best possible world, suggested that our universe might not be absolutely the best, but it will be uniquely good.[4] Perhaps all possible worlds exist in which the good outweighs the bad, for every sentient being that enjoys the good and fears the bad. But such a selection principle – 'a world exists for the sake of overwhelming and distinctive value' – would rule out many possible worlds that would be unbearably bad. That might well be thought a great advantage.

Weinberg, who is an atheist, refuses to think that a God who produced this universe, even if it is necessary for God to do so, is good. But we have seen that to call God good is to say that God actualizes in the divine being the highest degree of all compatible perfections. If such a God necessarily produces a universe like this, then God remains good, whatever the universe is like. A supremely good God might, then, necessarily create this universe, or some universe with similar characteristics.

Is This Universe Good?

The appeal to necessity is strong. But it is not quite enough. God, after all, creates the universe in order to actualize new forms of goodness. God could not produce an evil universe. Therefore we still have to ask whether the goods of this universe are sufficient to outweigh the evils.

What has been established is that a perfectly good God could create a universe with many evils in it – even that God could not create a universe with intelligent life without creating some evils. Yet if God creates for the sake of good, the evils cannot outweigh the goods.

Our universe develops from relatively simple initial conditions by a long process of emergent complexity. From it arise beings like us, who carry the inheritance of our evolutionary past with us – all our drives to selfishness and altruism, and all our passions and unactualized possibilities. We have the capacity to shape ourselves, to grow in community and to pursue values through creative effort. These are some of the distinctive goods that belong to our human form of life.

It follows, however, that we therefore also have the capacity to misshape ourselves, to break down community and to turn away from creative effort to the pursuit of easier pleasures. We are, in short, beings capable of moral and intellectual virtue, yet always in danger of misusing our potentialities for good.

This is a universe of distinctive sorts of good, which could only exist in an evolutionary, emergent, law-based universe. While we may not be the only possible forms of intelligent life, perhaps beings like us could only live in a universe with laws like the ones we have. And perhaps we would have to have the capacity to destroy and harm, which are the correlates of our capacity to create and co-operate.

This may not be the best of all possible worlds. But it may be the only universe that can actualize the sorts of values that we carbon-based life-forms can actualize. God may well desire such life-forms. In that case some evils must exist in our world. And the world necessarily carries the possibility of greater evils, if we misuse our freedom.

That is why evils exist in a world created by a supremely good God. This world does contain very great and otherwise unobtainable goods. But, given the postulate of God, we can say more. If God is the supremely perfect creator, God could not desire the existence of great evils, even though God could not prevent them from existing. Yet such a God might be able to ensure that no evil – no pain suffered by any sentient creature – was utterly useless, or without good effect, not only for the universe in general, but also for the suffering creature itself.

A perfectly good God would never desire suffering, but might perhaps be able to use suffering for the good of the sufferer as well as for others. I do not mean that suffering would ever be good in itself – that is a horrifying thought. But I do mean that suffering could be used to realize a form of good that otherwise would not have existed.

An example would be the way in which a self-sacrificial death could be the means of protecting many innocent people. But more is possible if God is the source of all existence. God could give the sufferer a new form of existence in which new sorts of good exist, for the sufferer herself, that have their precise character because of the suffering that has been endured. The suffering would then not have been in vain, though it could never be directly chosen as a means to a good end.

One of the most powerful statements of the problem of suffering is found in Dostoevsky's novel *The Brothers Karamazov.* Ivan Karamazov asks his brother Alyosha if he would consent to creating a universe with the object of making people happy in the end, if it was essential and inevitable to torture to death 'only one tiny creature' and 'to found that edifice on its unavenged tears'. Alyosha, a religious believer, softly replies that he would not consent.

Perhaps silence is the only response in the face of such suffering. Yet Ivan's question implies that the creator intends the suffering as a means to a good end, and this cannot be so. That suffering seems horrendous and unacceptable – and so it is. The creator never directly intends it. Insofar as it is the result of human action, the creator absolutely forbids it. If it is the result of the misuse of human freedom, nothing could justify it morally. Yet it may be the case that, given the laws of nature and human freedom, it could not have been prevented. The creator creates – and perhaps has to create – for the sake of good, but cannot prevent the occurrence of suffering, though the creator never intends it, and never creates it as a means to a good end. You may say the creator still bears responsibility for it. Perhaps the creator shares and experiences that suffering too. But the final and only justification must be that it is indeed unpreventable in any universe in which we exist. But if that was the whole story, we may well feel, like Ivan, that we would rather not exist at all than live in such a world.

Suppose, however – and this is part of the God hypothesis, not a new and unexpected way out of a difficult problem – that God could take the life of that creature, and place it in a world of supreme happiness and love for endless time. Suppose that creature could not otherwise have existed, and that its tears are not 'unavenged', for they are part of a continuing universe in which justice will reign, and all tears will be wiped away. And suppose that the suffering could be used to help others who have become lost in evil and despair – perhaps by assuring them that suffering is not the final word in finite lives, or perhaps by giving them some part in the creator's action for good in the world.

I am not saying this makes the suffering all right. I am not denying that it is horrendous. I am suggesting that the suffering need not be pointless; that God could transform it in a greater and wider reality so that it becomes part of a whole life and a wider community that, though tragic, yet realizes undeniable and unique forms of goodness.

If these things are possible, this strengthens the case for saying that the goods of creation outweigh its inevitable evils or its inevitable possibilities of evil. And that is a central part of the God hypothesis. All things come from God, and to God all things return. In the divine awareness of the world, its evils are qualified by their presence in the midst of overwhelming perfection. It is that divine awareness in which all finite sentient life can share. If this is true – and it is certainly possible, if there is a God – our world remains tragic, yet overwhelmingly good.

The Delusion of Materialism

But is our world like that? Or is this a delusion constructed to make human life bearable? If you are a materialist, you will be bound to think it is a delusion. Consciousness of any sort will be dependent upon matter, and it will not be possible for living beings to transfer to another sort of existence. There will not be a God, and there will not be a life after death.

But perhaps materialism is the greater delusion. Consciousness is the most evident sort of existence there is, and it is not necessarily bound to matter. It will then be very natural for finite consciousnesses to have an affinity with the spiritual consciousness of God, and sharing in the divine awareness is their most natural form of existence. The delusion is that consciousness does not exist, or that it wholly depends on matter. If we can establish conscious affinity with God, then it is likely that such affinity can endure beyond the death of our physical bodies. It is because we have affinity with God that immortality becomes a possibility and a reasonable hope.

Immortality is not a fiction invented to compensate for an unhappy life. It is the perception that our conscious lives are not bounded by this space and time, and that they find their fulfilment in union with a supreme spiritual reality that seems, even during this life, to take us beyond the limits of time.

If we have such a perception, we will see conscious life as the necessary condition of the creation and enjoyment of many kinds of good. We will see the whole history of the universe as directed towards the emergence of finite beings who can share in the conscious appreciation of such goods. And we will see the foundation of all reality in a supreme consciousness that creates worlds for the sake of the emergence of new sorts of goodness, which will vastly outweigh the evils that must inevitably result from such creation.

Scientific investigation will not provide such perception. It is a fundamental ontological stance, confirmed by the experience of millions of wise and good people. It provides a personal explanation for the cosmos, a form of explanation with which present science is not concerned.

The Collapse of the Boeing 747 Gambit

Dawkins says that the God hypothesis is 'a total abdication of the responsibility to find an explanation. It is a dreadful exhibition of self-indulgent, thought-denying skyhookery.'[5] I have shown that, on the contrary, the God hypothesis is a sustained attempt to find an explanation for why the universe is as it is. It is not an attempt to find a scientific explanation. It does not, or should not, compete with scientific explanation. In fact it should – and in its most famous classical exponents it does – motivate and inspire a continuing search for greater scientific understanding of the universe. That is because it postulates that the universe is created by a rational (wise) God who gives humans the ability and responsibility to understand it.

The main point on which Dawkins and I disagree is that there is an important sort of explanation that is not reducible to scientific explanation, but is complementary to it. That is personal explanation, in terms of consciousness, value and purpose. It is personal explanation that the God hypothesis proposes as the ultimate form of explanation. To propose such a form of explanation is not to abdicate responsibility, but to assert that thinkers such as Dawkins fail to see that scientific explanation is not the only form of explanation there is. To turn his own words back on him, he 'mistakes what it means to explain something'[6] in personal terms.

I cannot see that a rigorous defence of personal explanation (such as that given by American philosopher Richard Taylor)[7] is self-indulgent or that it is 'thought-denying'. It takes quite a lot of thinking to formulate it, and it is not self-indulgent if you do not particularly want to believe in God (perhaps because you dislike organized religions).

Is it 'skyhookery'? The term comes from Daniel Dennett, and it is a revealing use of a materialistic metaphor for understanding the universe. 'I am not advocating some sort of narrowly scientistic way of thinking,' Dawkins says.[8] But he immediately adds, 'The very least that any honest quest for truth must have in setting out to explain… a universe is a crane and not a skyhook.' But that is just what narrowly scientistic thinking is!

A 'crane' is a naturalistic explanation, in terms of preceding states and general mathematically expressible laws. A 'skyhook' is a hook dangling from the sky (where the skygod lives, of course) that pulls things up by some sort of magical or supernatural action, which is quite beyond the power of science to explain.

Since we know that there are no hooks hanging from the sky, and that there is no god in the sky, the point of the metaphor is to make us see how absurd the whole idea of skyhooks is. 'Skyhookery' is, I suppose, the belief that there are supernatural causes operative in the processes of nature. Where they exist, scientists are warned to keep out, since this is holy ground. But the status of such a belief is rather like belief in fairies, who are no more improbable than hooks dangling from thin air.

Those who believe that there is a final personal explanation for the universe do not believe that there are hooks dangling from the sky. We believe that mind – or something that is not less than mind, with consciousness, wisdom and purpose – is the ultimate reality, and that all physical processes exist for some good reason conceived by that mind. Most of us do not believe that the cosmic mind will enter into a scientific explanation, any more than it will enter into a manual of car mechanics. But we do believe that the existence of ultimate mind makes a difference to the world – to the world's elegance, beauty and intelligibility, for instance. And we do believe that the final explanation of the universe will take us beyond scientific explanation to the level of metaphysical explanation.

I would never adopt the motto: 'Let us have skyhooks instead of cranes.' But I would suggest that we need personal explanation in addition to scientific explanation if we are to understand the ultimate nature of reality, and if there is to be a truly final explanation of why the universe is as it is.

If this is allowed, even as a possibility, the Boeing 747 gambit collapses. The gambit was this: 'a designer god cannot be used to explain organized complexity because any God capable of designing anything would have to be complex enough to demand the same kind of explanation'.[9]

Here are six reasons why the gambit does not succeed. First, God is not complex in the way that material organisms are complex – made up of separate parts combined together. In fact God is simple in three main senses: God is one unitary consciousness; God is the one and only cause of all things other than God; and God acts on one general principle. Such a God does explain (raise the probability of) organized complexity, by providing a reason for its existence – the actualization of distinctive and otherwise unobtainable values.

Second, God, being not less than pure consciousness, demands a different kind of explanation than complex physical organisms do. God does not stand in need of 'the same kind of explanation' as organized physical complexity. There needs to be a different kind of explanation for the existence of one unitary primordial consciousness.

Third, that explanation is not in terms of probability. For it is not true that, with regard to the existence of universes and their laws, the simple is more probable than the complex. It is not true that God is less probable than the universe. And it is not true that the laws of probability forbid the existence of a necessary and eternal mind.

Fourth, any final explanation of a universe must somehow explain, or make virtually certain, its own existence. The relevant criteria for a final explanation are parsimony, elegance, comprehensiveness and – most importantly – necessity. Any entity that could be a final explanation would have to be eternal (and therefore uncausable and unchangeable in existence) and necessary (having no alternative to its existence). The God hypothesis posits an eternal and necessary mind, and this is the most intelligible location for the mathematical postulate of an eternal and necessary set of all possible universes from which this universe arises. So God meets the criteria for a final explanation very well, and better than the Darwinian algorithm, which, though illuminating and important, is far from being a final explanation, since it leaves a multiplicity of physical laws and states unexplained.

Fifth, the God hypothesis makes possible a simple and elegant reason for the existence of one or more universes, by proposing that they are actualized for the sake of their distinctive goodness. This proposal implies both that the being of God will be of supreme value in itself, and that any actual universe will be of great distinctive value.

Sixth, God can unify scientific and personal explanations in a harmonious way, without reducing one to the other. This proposal is superior to any hypothesis that simply eliminates either scientific law or the fact of consciousness from reality.

Thus, if there is a final rational explanation for the universe, God is the best candidate. The Boeing 747 gambit has failed. It was indeed, in the words of the Oxford English Dictionary's definition of a gambit, 'a trick or a ruse'.

Of course, I do not think that most people who believe in God do so because of such very abstract considerations. Nevertheless, these considerations show that the God hypothesis is a deeply rational, coherent and plausible one. They form the intellectual background for a number of other arguments for God, generally more familiar to people, which Dawkins says are 'spectacularly weak'. Armed with the results of my analysis so far, I will now show that, on the contrary, they are remarkably strong, and that Dawkins' 'easy exposure' of them as vacuous misses his target by a considerable distance.

Part 3

On Chapter Three
of *The God Delusion*

6

The Five Ways

The Five Ways of Thomas Aquinas

Although they are not by any means the only arguments for God's existence, Thomas Aquinas' 'Five Ways in which one can prove that there is a God' are perhaps the best known. Dawkins claims that they are easily exposed as vacuous, and he does so in just three pages. This would be a very impressive achievement, except that he does not in fact deal with Aquinas' Five Ways at all. What he does is to consider instead five arguments of his own, which bear a vague resemblance to those of Aquinas – in some cases, a resemblance so vague that it can no longer be recognized.

Aquinas cannot really be understood without reference to Aristotle, whose arguments Aquinas is in effect repeating. That requires a great deal of technical expertise in ancient Greek philosophy. Because Aristotle's philosophy has been considered many times by many experts, I shall not repeat the exercise, and Dawkins does not do so either.

I want to follow Dawkins' method, and propound five arguments of my own. My main excuse for this is that I will thereby be doing just what Thomas Aquinas was doing in his day – using the best available science to explore the question of what the most adequate final explanation of the universe might be.

In the thirteenth century, Aristotle was considered by many scholars to be the greatest scientific authority. Aquinas' use of Aristotle was thought by some to be radical and innovatory – some of Aquinas' opinions were condemned by the Bishop of Paris in 1277.

The trouble with using Aristotle is that we now know that most of Aristotle's opinions about physics were mistaken. Nevertheless, he was an outstanding early scientist, and I will maintain that modern science can be used to justify the same general sorts of conclusions that Aquinas drew from Aristotle. So I will rephrase the Five Ways in the light of modern science.

If you are interested in Aquinas' own formulation, it can be found in his great work the *Summa Theologiae*.[1] It will be obvious that the arguments are quite different from the ones Dawkins considers. I too am going to formulate Aquinas' arguments in a rather different way, but a way that is much more sympathetic to Aquinas' intentions.

I should first say something about what a 'proof of God' might be. A valid proof cannot contain more in the conclusion than was implicit in the premises, even though the conclusion may be psychologically surprising or unexpected. If you reject the premises and axioms of a proof, then clearly it will not prove anything to you. It is a matter of thinking whether you really do accept the premises, and then of seeing whether the suggested implications of that acceptance are as the proof says.

The Five Ways only have a hope of working if we accept the unstated first premises that the universe is an intelligible and rational structure, and that the search for a final, ultimately satisfying explanation of that is a rational and proper search. What each proof does is to elucidate one implication of those premises in order to build up a picture of what a final rational explanation of the universe will be.

An important background to the Five Ways is thus a consideration of what sorts of explanation for the universe there might be. In particular, serious consideration of the arguments of the Five Ways requires acceptance that personal explanation is a proper and irreducible form of explanation, and that the existence of an ultimate mind as the source of all reality is a coherent and plausible notion.

So the Five Ways can be seen as articulations of the idea of ultimate mind as the final personal explanation of the universe. If that idea is dismissed at the outset, the proofs cannot succeed. But if the idea is accepted as a real possibility, then the proofs both provide more detailed specifications of the idea, and provide good reasons for accepting that the idea corresponds to reality – that there is a God.

The First and Second Ways of Proving God

Bearing all that in mind, the 'First Way' involves an analysis of the idea of efficient causality. For Aristotle, an efficient cause is not, as in some more recent philosophy, just a state that precedes some other state and is regularly connected to it by some general law. An efficient cause actually brings about its effect. As Aquinas puts it, the cause moves some state from possibility, or potential existence, into actual existence.

Since nothing can move itself from possibility to actuality, everything that changes is changed by something else. An infinite regress of causes would leave the universe without a final explanation. So if this universe consists of chains of causes going back to one originative event (which it does), and if there is a final explanation of the universe, there must be some cause of the whole series of changes which is immutable, not capable of being changed by anything else.

This 'unchanged changer' would not have to be immutable in every respect. It could change itself, or allow itself to be changed by beings it had created. But something essential to its nature could not be changed – for instance, its existence as a being capable of causing changes.

We can say a little more than this. If it is to be truly explanatory, the first cause must in some way contain in itself the parameters and goals of all future changes. As the ultimate cause of all future changes, it will contain the potentiality for all of them.

In Question 4 of Article 2, Aquinas says, 'Effects obviously pre-exist potentially in their causes.' What he has in mind is that effects cannot be radically novel, wholly unpredictable or totally unforeseeable by any observing mind. If they were, the universe would be unintelligible. So in some way the first cause must contain the potentiality for all its possible effects.

The first cause of the universe will be immutable in existence and general nature, and will in some sense contain a specification of all possible future states that it may produce. From a knowledge of its nature – which it alone may fully possess – all possible changes in all possible universes can be inferred.

It is the appeal, left implicit in Aquinas, to mind as the conceiver of possibilities that enables us to understand how a cause can contain its effects 'potentially' and 'in a higher manner'. A mind can 'contain' its effect by having an idea of it. Such an idea is the potentiality of the actual thing.

For Aquinas, if all states that come into being are made actual by something actual that contains the idea of their potentiality, then there must be at least one actual state that does not come into being. The simplest hypothesis is that there is one unchanging mind that contains all potential states of the universe. All possible states will exist in this unchanging mind, and it is in that way that all effects pre-exist potentially in one ultimate mind.

The 'Second Way' amplifies this argument by drawing attention not just to change, but to the origin or coming into being of things. Everything, says Aquinas, that comes into being is brought into being by something else. Modern science is founded on this postulate – that every event has a cause. So though it could be denied, nobody with a scientific inclination would deny it.

Again, if there is to be a final explanation, there cannot be an infinite regress of causes. So there must be some 'first cause'. That first cause does not just happen not to come into being. It could not possibly come into being, because it is timeless or eternal. No timeless being can be brought into being or caused, since there is no previous time in which it ever was not.

So the first two ways seek to persuade us that, if the universe has a final explanation, it will lie in an eternal, immutable being that contains the potentiality for all possible states within itself – and that means the specification of all possible states plus the power to actualize such states.

Dawkins does not think much of these two ways. He thinks they 'arbitrarily conjure up a terminator to an infinite regress' and then give it a name. But, he says, to think that God is immune to the regress is 'an entirely unwarranted assumption'.[2]

His mistake is to think that God, the ultimate terminator, is the same sort of thing as the members of the infinite regress of changers or causes. But if the regress is of 'things moving from potentiality to actuality', or of things 'coming into being', then it is clearly possible that there could be something that was never potential and that is not in time. This entity would not be part of the regress, but it could possibly be the cause of such a regress.

When quantum physicists speak of this space-time universe as originating by quantum fluctuations in a vacuum, they are positing just such a move to account for things in space-time by referring to a supra-space-time entity (quantum laws and the vacuum energy state). The God hypothesis postulates a supra-space-time entity of a mental sort that contains all quantum laws and energy potentials. Even if you do not accept it, this is not an arbitrary supposition. If you start by accepting that such a primordial mind is possible, and that the universe could well have a final explanation, the first two ways of Aquinas give good reasons for thinking that the primordial mind is also actual, that God exists.

The Third Way

Dawkins claims that Aquinas' 'Third Way' just says the same thing as the first two ways. Possibly he thinks this because he has not read it. Certainly the version of it he gives in his book is nothing like Aquinas' argument (which, of course, comes from Aristotle).

Aquinas' argument is actually about the possibility of necessary existence, or of 'what must be'. The heart of it is the claim that, if everything in the universe is contingent, then there might well have been nothing at all. But to suppose that the universe could originate from nothing is to give up all hope of a final explanation. So a truly final explanation must postulate the existence of a first cause that is necessary, that could not fail to exist or to be other than it is.

Some recent writers on science, such as Peter Atkins in his book *Creation Revisited*,[3] which Dawkins refers to as his favourite work of scientific prose poetry, speak of the universe as originating out of nothing. I too think that Atkins' book is beautifully written, but it is partly poetry. One of its poetic features is Atkins' use of the word 'nothing' to mean 'huge numbers of very complicated things'.

The 'nothing' that Atkins postulates is a very precise balancing of fundamental forces, such as gravitational and inflationary force. Because these forces are, respectively, negative and positive, they balance each other out, and add up to zero energy. But this is rather like saying that, if I have a million pounds in one bank, and I owe another bank a million pounds, I have nothing. In one sense this is true. But in fact I have two bank accounts, and lots of money and debts. That is very different from being a penniless tramp, and I will certainly be treated very differently. I will probably be treated better by the bank manager to whom I owe a million pounds, in the hope that he will get his money back.

So Atkins' 'nothing' ceaselessly produces scintillations of particles and energy, as universes flash in and out of existence. And these scintillations are all governed by quantum laws of an amazingly complex and elegant sort. That is, it must be said, a very busy and complex and active sort of nothing.

Atkins has on at least one occasion (after a public debate with me) confessed to being a sort of mathematical Platonist. He thinks universes originate from a quasi-mathematical realm that has the kind of necessity possessed by mathematical truths. The ultimate quantum laws and balance of fundamental forces is somehow necessarily what it is.

If we could show that some being or state was absolutely necessary, that only one set of axioms derived from it could give rise to a universe of intelligent life-forms like us, and that some derivation of that sort necessarily arises from the original state, then we would have a final explanation for the universe. It would be the 'final theory' of which Steven Weinberg once dreamed, and which drives the cosmological quest for a Theory of Everything.

Whether or not a Theory of Everything will prove to be possible in cosmology, it has long been a postulate of classical theology that there is an ultimately necessary being from which the universe derives. Far from being an arbitrary stopping point, that is the natural terminus of a belief in the final intelligibility of the universe.

Taken together, as they must be, the first three ways show that if the universe is completely intelligible, it must have a final explanation. That explanation will lie in the postulation of a being that is immutable, eternal and necessary, and that contains all possible derived states in its own being.

The Third Way is what Immanuel Kant called 'the cosmological argument',[4] and Kant is sometimes said to have undermined the argument by stating that anything at all might be necessary, for all we know. So the argument does not prove anything like an all-perfect God – for which, he argued, the ontological argument would be needed.

Of course, no particular argument for God establishes everything we want to know about God. This argument only establishes necessity; but what Kant overlooks is that it has to be the necessity of a being that explains the universe, and therefore it could not be, for example, a necessary frog or a necessary and eternal banana. It has to be a being that contains all possible states and a reason for actualizing some or all of them. It has to be what Kant himself actually postulated, a necessary and eternal mind.

Kant's other main argument was taken from David Hume: we can always imagine God not existing, so God cannot be necessary.[5] The decisive answer to this is the one that Hume himself gave elsewhere in his writings: 'Human understanding... is by no means fitted for such remote and abstruse subjects',[6] and 'The ultimate springs and principles [of nature] are totally shut up from human curiosity and inquiry'.[7]

What human beings can imagine or picture to themselves is not a reliable guide to the ultimate nature of reality. So the fact that we can imagine God not existing does not show that God, as God actually is, might not have existed.

In fact, Hume's most basic claim is that we cannot decide what is ultimately real simply by calling up mental images. Hume vastly underestimated the capacity of human understanding to uncover the hidden structure of the cosmos. Pure mathematical thought, when tested by observation, does seem to be a good guide to what is real. But mathematical thought is very different from just calling up mental pictures or images. And when we are dealing with God, it is to be expected that the nature of God far surpasses any possibility of complete comprehension by human minds. So it is just not good enough to claim that, since I seem to be able to picture a world without God, there could actually be one. How could I possibly know that I have coherently conceived of such a world, when its ultimate structure is not known to me?

Hume is right in thinking that we cannot prove that a necessary being exists just by claiming to conceive or frame the idea of one (for instance, as 'a being that exists in every possible world'). That is the ontological argument, and most philosophers accept that it does not work.

It looks as though I can conceive both that there is a being that exists in all possible worlds, and that there is some possible world in which that being does not exist. These cannot both be right, so how do I decide between them? What Kant actually says is that if I am committed to the intelligibility of the universe, then I am committed to the existence of a final explanation. That in turn commits me to the existence of a necessary cause of all. The decision is made by my practical commitment to scientific method and to the intelligibility of the universe.

Kant calls this a postulate of practical reason rather than a proof by theoretical reason. It is quite false to say that Kant has undermined the cosmological argument for God. Closer reading shows that he merely objects to a theoretical, verifiable proof that will convince anyone beyond reasonable doubt. He accepts that the postulate of a necessary eternal mind as the cause of all is the only logically adequate termination of the quest for a final explanation of the universe. In this he is surely right.

An Interlude on Dawkins' Alleged Paradox

In the course of his discussion of an argument to necessity that does not bear much relation to the one Aquinas actually gives, Dawkins takes a moment to say, 'It has not escaped the notice of logicians that omniscience and omnipotence are mutually incompatible.'[8] He makes it sound as though all logicians are agreed on this point. I have asked all the logicians I know (once upon a time, I taught logic myself, but I may have forgotten what I thought before I went to seed and became a theologian), and they do not think that what Dawkins says is true.

There are difficulties about framing definitions of 'omniscience' and 'omnipotence' that are compatible with each other, but most logicians can manage it well enough. It is in fact a good introductory exercise in systematic theology. But since Dawkins remarks, 'I have yet to see any good reason to suppose that theology is a subject at all,'[9] it would hardly be surprising if he had not noticed that any such exercises exist.

It would be a mistake to think that there is universal agreement about definitions of the divine attributes. There are quite a few different proposals. The God hypothesis, as formulated by Dawkins and agreed by me, does not mention either omniscience or omnipotence. It only speaks of 'superhuman intelligence'. But if we think of the eternal necessary mind postulated by the first three ways, we might say that the mind must have knowledge of all possible states of affairs, and presumably also of the actual states it produces out of those possibilities. That is one sense of 'omniscience' – knowing all possibles and all actuals that are produced. It must also be able to produce enough actual states to include our universe and any other universe that might exist. That is one sense of 'omnipotence' – being the only source of the existence of actual universes.

These may seem to be relatively restricted definitions. Some medieval theologians expanded them considerably. They took omniscience to entail knowledge of the truth-value of every proposition, past, present or future. Omnipotence, they thought, entailed the ability to bring about any state that could be described in a consistent proposition.

Those expanded definitions cause the trouble Dawkins refers to. It looks as though God can know the future, and then change his mind, thereby proving himself wrong, and so causing big logical trouble. But the medieval theologians were very acute logicians, and readily produced many ways of making the definitions consistent. Resolving the alleged contradiction is easy. An eternal being cannot logically change its mind, so it is no restriction on omnipotence that God cannot change his mind. Even an omnipotent being cannot do what is logically impossible.

That resolves the issue of contradiction. But as a matter of fact I prefer an alternative solution. I am more sympathetic to Dawkins' point. The point is that a truly omnipotent being should be able to do new, original, creative things. Creativity and originality are great values, and it would be good for God to possess them. This is a value-judgment that, surprisingly perhaps, only became widespread after the sixteenth century in Europe. Possibly it reflects the growing interest in the ability of technology to change the world for the better, whereas before that it was often assumed that all change was for the worse. As the Duke of Wellington once said, 'Reform? Reform? Aren't things bad enough already?'

As I have previously argued, a being that is necessary in existence and in its essential nature could also be creatively free in many of its particular actions. If it is good for God to be creatively free, then it could well be necessarily true that God is creatively free.

If God is creatively free, then God can 'change his mind'. In that case, omniscience must be taken to mean that God knows everything it is logically possible for any being to know. But no possible being could know what it has not yet decided, or perhaps what it has allowed other beings to decide freely. So there is still no problem with making omniscience and omnipotence consistent.

It is perfectly reasonable to adopt a definition of omniscience such that 'knowing everything possible' does not include things not yet decided (since that is not possible), and to adopt a definition of omnipotence such that 'being able to do everything possible' does not include being able to do things that conflict with the necessary nature of God (like unutterably evil things).

Then we could say that there are necessary limits on the things God, as an ultimately necessary being, can do. God cannot do absolutely anything. But since we do not know the inner nature of God, we cannot know exactly what the limits of divine necessity are. Presumably God cannot commit suicide, or do evil for its own sake, or change the past. God is nevertheless omnipotent, because God is the only source of all finite existence, and can do the maximum that any possible being can do. What God cannot do is laid down by the necessities of the divine nature, which no possible being could evade. That is as much as we could reasonably ask of a definition of omnipotence.

God also knows everything it is possible for any being to know. But that cannot logically include things that God has not decided yet. And that seems as much as we could reasonably ask of a definition of omniscience. So it is not so easy to detect contradictions in the definition of God, though it is very easy to construct definitions that are contradictory, if that is what you want to do. What you should *not* say is that these are the 'real' definitions, and that all believers in God should really accept them, because all believers in God are so stupid that they ought to believe as many contradictions as they possibly can.

The Fourth Way

Dawkins' dismissal of the 'Fourth Way' only takes a paragraph. At least if he taught theology his course would have the advantage of being the shortest one in the university. In Aquinas this is an argument based on consideration of values. It marks a decisive turn in the Five Ways from scientific explanation to personal explanation. The first three ways concentrated on efficient causality, on the origin of the universe. They sought a first efficient cause that would fully account for why things in the universe are the way they are. They postulated an immutable, eternal and necessary mind, containing the ideas of all possible worlds, as the source of a fully intelligible cosmos.

The final two ways turn to consider what Aristotle called 'final causality' – that for the sake of which things exist. Such causality has long been excluded from natural science, as being outside its favoured and tested forms of explanation. Yet, in personal explanations, it plays a vital and apparently irreducible role.

We explain the acts of a personal being by identifying what it desires or values and then tries to obtain. If we try to reconstruct Aquinas' argument in these terms, we might say that an eternal mind that knows all possibilities, and has the power to choose some of them, will be able to discriminate between more or less desirable or valuable possibilities.

It will, if it has the power, choose for itself desirable rather than undesirable states. Moreover, it will choose states of the highest possible value. So it will be a being of supreme value, realizing in itself the maximal degree of beauty, happiness, wisdom, knowledge and creative freedom.

Insofar as these are timeless choices, they will simply follow from the divine nature itself, and will not (as in the human case) be choices that follow a process of knowledge and decision in temporal sequence. They follow necessarily from the divine nature. But they can be spoken of as 'choices' because they arise through knowledge and intention, rather than blindly or accidentally.

I myself think, in a post-Hegelian revision of the classical God hypothesis, that a timeless mind, incapable of coming into being or changing in its essential nature, may also have a temporal aspect. Indeed, I think that, if it is supremely perfect (valuable), it will necessarily have a temporal aspect. That is, it will timelessly generate a realm in which it can be freely creative in its choice of specific beauties and forms of happiness and knowledge. It will be unchangeably supreme in value, but the specific values it realizes may vary at particular times. Time, even within the divine being itself, may be, as Plato described it in his dialogue *Timaeus*, a 'moving image of eternity'.[10]

Whether you take the more classical view or the post-Hegelian view, the Fourth Way makes explicit that eternal mind will not only contain all possible states of affairs. It will discriminate between them, and choose to realize in itself the highest forms of value. It will be the supreme Good, worthy of admiration and reverence for its unique perfection.

That, I think, is a modern formulation of the Fourth Way. But in its original, its form of argument is much more Platonic. It relies on the axioms that all effects must pre-exist in their causes, and that the causes must be 'greater' or more perfect than their effects. Thus God's perfect goodness must be the cause of all the finite forms of goodness we see in things around us.

It is these axioms that Dawkins mocks. There are lots of smelly people around, he says. So they must all be ultimately caused by 'a pre-eminently peerless stinker, and we call him God'.[11] I have to admit that this made me laugh out loud. But of course Aquinas believes that

God is not physical in any sense. So God is not supremely smelly. In what sense, then, can smells pre-exist in God, especially in a 'greater' or 'higher' manner?

Plato, at one point in his dialogue *The Republic*, says that the idea of perfect Bedness, which exists in the world of Forms, Essences, or Ideas, is 'more real' than any actual physical beds.[12] So perhaps the idea of perfect Smelliness is more real than this-worldly stinks, which are actually only the appearances of stinks.

This Platonic way of thinking is very hard for us to get into. For us, physical particulars are obviously more real than ideas, which we see as abstractions. To understand Plato we need to go back to a different world-view, in which Ideas in the mind of God are more real than physical things, which are only imperfect appearances of the Ideas.

So what exists in the mind of God is the *idea* of the perfect stink. It is more of a possible stink than an actual stink. Is it more real than a physical stink? Only in the sense that the possible stink would still exist, would eternally exist, even if there were no actual physical stinks at all. The possible stink shares in the being of God; it has a share in eternity – though of course it does not realize that. Actual stinks only last for a short while, thankfully, and they may not even exist at all.

I doubt if many of us can fully return to a Platonic world-view. But we can still understand how physical smells can be ultimately caused by a necessary and eternal mind that has in it the ideas of all possible smells, and the power to make them actual at an appropriate time and place. God is not the pre-eminent stinker. But God thinks of all possible stinks. If God finds some smells desirable, God may will them to exist. But it is not possible for a physical smell to exist within the being of God, since God is not physical. Whatever perfections the divine being contains, they will be purely spiritual or intellectual.

So the Fourth Way establishes that, if there is an eternal mind, it will contain all supreme spiritual values, and the ideas of all possible physical values. God is not just an object of intellectual satisfaction. God is also an object of true worship, which is reverence for supreme goodness just for its own sake.

The Fifth Way

Dawkins construes the 'Fifth Way' as holding that things look as though they have been designed, and so they must have been designed.[13] Put in that way, the argument falls to the Darwinian demonstration that natural selection working on genetic mutations can produce adaptations that look designed, but are not.

However, that is not quite the point of the argument. The basis of the argument in Aquinas is acceptance of the best scientific world-view available in his day, that of Aristotle. For Aristotle all substances (things) have four sorts of causes: a material cause (what the substance is made of); a formal cause (the essential nature of the substance); an efficient cause (what brings the substance into being); and a final cause (that for the sake of which the substance exists).

The Fifth Way is concerned with the idea of final causes. Aristotle held that every substance has a goal, a state that fulfils its proper potentiality, towards which it tends by its nature. This sort of goal-directedness is just part of the nature of things. It is not designed or intended by anyone.

Aristotle does speak of God as a being of supreme perfection, whose 'life is like the best that we can enjoy'.[14] But God is not actively concerned with the world, being wrapped in eternal contemplation of its own perfection. As Dante said in the *Divine Comedy*, God moves the sun and other stars by love. For Aristotle this means that substances love the supreme Good and try to imitate it in their own proper fashion. They have a sort of natural inner attraction to the Good, but the Good remains alone and indifferent to them.

Aquinas' argument is that it does not make sense to speak of inanimate objects 'loving' the Good, or trying to imitate it. The sort of goal-directedness they have is only intelligible if some being with awareness and understanding orders them towards their goal. The argument is not from the appearance of design. It is from the goal-directedness of all things to the necessity of design – the argument being that goals must be foreseen and intended by some conscious being if they are to exist.

In the sixteenth century, Aristotelian belief that all substances have final causes, that there is something for the sake of which they exist, was dropped from science. That may seem to be the end of the Fifth Way. But it is not. The idea of purposes in nature is an attractive and natural one, and it will not go away. It is of course an idea to which Dawkins is deeply opposed. In a strange sense, he agrees with Aquinas that if there is not a conscious awareness and understanding, there can be no real purposes. But he denies that there can be any awareness prior to the existence of matter. Therefore there can at best be the appearance of purpose in nature.

Suppose, however, that the first four ways have established that there is an eternal mind of supreme perfection, the one and only cause of the universe. Then that mind might well desire the existence of the finite goods that only a physical universe could provide. And it might well think that the existence of a finite, conscious being that could share in the creation and enjoyment of such goods is also desirable.

In that case any universe created by God would have a purpose, or a number of purposes. Those purposes would be the intrinsically desirable values for the sake of which the universe exists. They would explain why the universe exists.

They might include the existence of intelligible and elegant laws, together with a rich and complex variety of interesting and beautiful forms. The universe might be, as Leibniz put it, 'the means of obtaining as much variety as possible, but with the greatest order possible'.[15]

And the universe might, by a process of self-organizing complexification and development, generate intelligent conscious beings that could understand and to some extent co-operate in shaping the universe itself. They could grow in understanding and creative ability, and in communal responsibility. This would facilitate a great increase in the number and variety of goods that a supreme mind might desire and intend.

Bearing all this in mind, it becomes wholly reasonable to think that the appearance of wisdom and purpose in the universe is not illusory. The appearance is certainly there, and it is not wholly accounted for on Darwinian principles. Darwin's algorithm does not address the question of why the laws of nature are as elegant and intelligible as they are, or how it is that they are so precisely fine-tuned for the generation of intelligent life (that is what I earlier called the 'New Design Argument'). And the principles of physical mutation and selection do not account for the emergence of consciousness and intelligence as new factors in the universe with the amazing capacity to enable some finite organisms, to some extent, to escape from 'the tyranny of the selfish replicators'.[16]

A physical process may be said to be purposive if it is efficiently and elegantly ordered to the generation of a distinctive good. By this test, this universe looks like a purposive process. It may not be the case, as Aristotle thought, that all substances have final causes. But the universe itself may have a final cause, a goal to which it tends and for the sake of which it exists. That goal is the realization of distinctive sorts of goodness. The Fifth Way converges on this conclusion from two directions. First, if there is an eternal mind containing the potentiality for all possible universes, then it is a good reason for the existence of a universe that it generates a distinctive sort of good. Second, if the laws of nature look amazingly fine-tuned for life, elegant and intelligible, and if they generate conscious beings who can create and appreciate many sorts of value, then it is a reasonable hypothesis that a primordial being with awareness and understanding has envisaged those laws and values, and acted intentionally to bring them about.

The Five Ways of Thomas Aquinas are formulated in what is now an antique philosophical genre, though it is an intellectually profound and fascinating one. They are not easily exposed as vacuous. They are capable of reformulation in a more modern scientific context. When that is attempted, they provide very good reasons for accepting the God hypothesis – now expanded to provide the idea of one immutable, eternal mind of supreme value that exists by necessity and brings the universe into being for the best possible reason, for the sake of its goodness.

If there is a final explanation for the universe, and if the idea of a primordial mind is consistent and coherent, the Five Ways do a pretty good job of demonstrating the existence of God.

I can understand that Dawkins might deny both these things. I cannot understand why he should say that the five proofs 'don't prove anything'.[17] No one has to accept the premises of any proof. But proofs may still be surprising and illuminating. They are certainly exercises in rational and critical thought of a high order. They deserve rather more than the three pages it takes for Dawkins to dismiss them. That is partly (but it is only a small part of) why theology faculties exist.

The Ontological Argument

I do not have much to say about the ontological argument. I accept Dawkins' main point, as Thomas Aquinas did, that you cannot establish the existence of something just by the analysis of concepts. Aquinas says that God does exist necessarily, and this means that if we understood the nature of God completely, we would see (we could 'prove') that God must exist. But we do not understand the nature of God fully, and we certainly cannot establish the existence of God just by analysis of the idea of God that we have.[18]

What is interesting about the argument is that it successfully manages to construct an idea of God from one simple axiomatic definition. That definition, given by Anselm in the eleventh century, is that God is 'that than which nothing greater (more perfect) can be conceived'.[19]

The definition leaves many choices to be made of what we think is perfect. Obviously our idea of God will depend on our basic moral, intellectual and aesthetic values. If our idea of such values changes, then our idea of God will change correlatively. So we should expect that, while nearly all theists will accept Anselm's definition, there will be many disagreements about what a perfect being would be.

Anselm thought that a perfect being would be strictly changeless, since any change from perfection would be for the worse. I have accepted that a perfect being must be changeless in some sense – in existence and in being perfect, most obviously. But since the eighteenth century change has come to many philosophers to seem a perfection. It is the condition of creative freedom and creativity, which are good things. If so, a perfect being would be changeless in some respects and changeable in others, without ever getting better or worse overall.

Relationship is another perfection that people have disagreed about. Aristotle thought that a perfect God would not be related to others, since if the relationship broke down, that would import change and possible imperfection into God. But many Christian theologians have argued that relationship makes possible self-giving love and co-operation, which are perfections. These perfections would entail the possibility of imperfection (of suffering, for example), but the imperfections might never become actual, and would be outweighed by the perfection of love. Here, too, there is scope for disagreement about the relative importance of various values – though few would dispute that they are all values, if not in God then in the finite realm.

The ontological argument claims that 'necessary existence' – the property of being uncausable and indestructible – would be an essential property of a perfect being. As Aquinas puts it, existence would be part of the essence of the perfect being. God exists more fully than anything else, and to think of God not existing is not to think properly of God.

I think this is correct. If we could understand God truly, we would see that it is impossible for God not to exist. God is the fullness of being, and all other things are derived, partial and imperfect expressions of the divine being. When thinking of what God is, it is important to see God not as a personal mind who happens to exist, but as the fullness of existence itself, whose being dazzles by excess of light, and who is more perfect than anything we can imagine.

Anselm's lucid definition is important in making this clear. But it still does not show that God actually exists. It shows that God is either necessary (God cannot fail to exist) or impossible (that the concept is incoherent). But we cannot, simply by thinking, establish which.

The function of the ontological argument, then, is not to prove God, but to remind us of the uniqueness and incomparability of the divine being. It spells out what it is to be a being of supreme perfection. Kant was wrong in thinking that it is the foundation of all theoretical arguments for God.[20] On the contrary, we arrive at it by way of considering what a final personal explanation would be, and determining that it would lie in a being who existed both by necessity and because it is supremely good that it should exist. That is a postulate of reason. It is elegant, economical and attractive. But to affirm its objective reality we need confirmation of some sort from experience. As in science, elegant speculation needs some sort of confirmation from experience. That confirmation may be difficult to determine, and it may not be wholly free of ambiguity. But in the end it will be what leads most people to positive belief in God. It is therefore important to investigate its nature and its possibility.

The Argument from Personal Experience

Part 1: Visions and Voices

When Dawkins deals with arguments for God that are based on personal experience, he mentions only mistaking a bird call for the voice of the devil, visions of angels or virgins, and hearing voices in the head. These, he suggests, are rather like seeing pink elephants, or like the Yorkshire Ripper hearing Jesus tell him to kill women. He quotes Sam Harris: 'While religious people are not generally mad, their core beliefs absolutely are.'[1]

Then he points out that the brain has simulation software that is 'well capable of constructing visions and visitations'. The wind can be heard as a murmuring voice, and curtains can be seen as a malign face. And he says, 'That is really all that needs to be said about personal experiences of gods or other religious phenomena.'[2]

I suppose if you are wholly convinced that there is no primordial mind of supreme value and no spiritual reality underlying the sensory appearances of the material world, then you are bound to regard all alleged apprehensions of such a spiritual reality as illusions and misinterpretations. That is why it is important to have arguments for God, good reasons for thinking that there may be an ultimate reality of supreme value. Such arguments will only lead to belief in God for a few intellectuals. Still, they serve to demonstrate that God is a real option, a perfectly rational, and indeed supremely rational, candidate for the role of ultimate reality.

If you think this is even a good possibility, you will expect to find some genuine personal apprehensions of God, who is, after all, a spiritual presence at every place and time.

What will such apprehensions be like? They will not be much like meeting another finite person, as though God was just an invisible humanoid. We are thinking of an immutable, eternal, necessary ground of all possibilities, of maximal spiritual beauty, wisdom and goodness, who holds all finite things in being for the sake of their distinctive goodness. How on earth can a human relate to such an omniscient, omnipotent, omnipresent pure Spirit?

It seems clear that it will not primarily be through such things as visions and voices in the head. For such visions and voices to be taken as manifestations of God, you would already have to be able to interpret them as communications from a supreme Spirit. Visions of pink elephants are not usually interpreted in that way. And since they usually occur after consuming large amounts of alcohol, it is very unlikely that they would be disclosures of ultimate reality. We have no reason to think that the ultimate reality is a pink elephant, any more than it is a turtle. And we have many reasons for thinking that people get less coherent and reliable when drunk.

If we think of a religious vision, such as an apparition of the Virgin Mary or an angel, there is reason to take this as a communication from God, since in some religious traditions they have played an important spiritual role as mediators of God. If we are not drunk or otherwise mentally impaired, we have to allow that the apparitions may be genuine. If, as in the case of the Ripper, they tell us to do something immoral or unintelligible, that is a good reason for denying their genuineness. God – at least the God that I and most philosophers and theologians talk about – is rational and supremely good. So no irrational or immoral suggestion could come from God.

Apparitions are, as Dawkins says, constructed by our brain-simulation software. But that does not mean they are not genuine. In the cinema, the brain simulates a continuous flowing film from a quick succession of still pictures. But it thereby constructs a genuine copy of a continuous flow of actions that did happen. So the brain may construct a vision of the Virgin Mary, looking just as she looks in the pictures we have seen, and dressed in just the clothes we expect. But this is not like 'seeing' a face in the curtains, or 'hearing' a voice in the wind. It is not, or at least it may not be, a misinterpretation of some visual array that is really something else. We may check the curtains carefully, and listen closely. And the apparition may still be there.

It is because most visions take forms familiar in a specific religious tradition that it seems they are largely mind-constructed. They may not be seen by others who are nearby. But that does not mean they have no objectivity. Such mind-constructed visions, often shared by many but not all minds, may convey a real spiritual presence in sensory forms that human minds can 'visualize' or 'hear'.

One vision that I accept is the resurrection of Jesus. According to the New Testament accounts, that apparently took the form of a visionary, temporary physical form that appeared and disappeared in a locked room, or walked unrecognized for seven miles, or manifested as a blinding light on the road to Damascus. These visions were of a uniquely 'solid' form, involving (if we take the accounts seriously) the ability to eat, walk and conduct a conversation. Yet their visionary character is made obvious by their transient and discontinuous nature (the appearances did not last long, and they began and ended abruptly). This was an objective series of visions, manifesting a real spiritual presence in physical form, and thereby conveying important spiritual truth to those who saw it.

We know that there are many fraudulent claims to have seen apparitions. There are many cases of people who hear voices telling them to do terrible things. There are many people who are deluded into thinking they have been abducted by extra-terrestrials or are really Napoleon. So we are wise to be careful. But if there are fraudulent and deluded claims, it is logically possible that there could be genuine claims by people who are not immoral, or who are not in general 'mad' (suffering from mental beliefs that make them unable to run their lives effectively or happily).

If there are genuine communications from God by means of mind-constructed visual images or 'words', we might also want to say that the information they convey should extend knowledge and should have important spiritual significance. If the Virgin Mary just said, 'The cigars up here are great,' we might well wonder if we were not, after all, having a vivid daydream. But if she said, 'I am alive and will pray for you,' that might convey the significant truth that those who have died on earth (or at least some of them) do exist in some form after death and do care about us.

I am not saying that all visions of the Virgin are genuine. Nevertheless, having made as many reality checks as we can, we must conclude that a claim to see an apparition made by a sane, moral, rational, critically aware and trustworthy person has to be considered a candidate for a genuine communication of truth from God. That is only so if belief in God is not 'mad'. It has to be a reasonable postulate. If it is, it may well be confirmed by visions or voices.

In most religions, some visions or inspired words are considered to be 'revelations'. This is a rare and definitive communication of important spiritual and moral truth from God, through a human intermediary or prophet. It seems highly probable that, if there is a God, there will be some such communication of God's nature and purpose. There will be revelation, or a finite communication of divine truth through a medium of great beauty, wisdom, moral insight and spiritual power. It may be a text or a person, or a text communicated through a person who has an especially close relationship to God.

Again, we have to judge as well as we can whether a person has such a close relationship to God. We will examine their lives for moral heroism, inspired wisdom, spiritual peace and joy, a sense of union with the supreme Spirit, and liberation from self. But it is reasonable to think that some humans will have an especially close and intense knowledge and love of God, or that God will take some human lives and unite them closely to the divine in knowledge and love. They will become the channels of divine revelation of what God is and of what God desires for us and for the world.

Dawkins at one point quotes American biologist James Watson as saying, 'I can't believe anyone accepts truth by revelation.'[3] That is only because he thinks it is very, very improbable that there is a God who might reveal anything. But if you think it is reasonable to see God as the only ultimate reality (as it is), then you will also think it is reasonable for God to reveal spiritual truth through prophets whose minds God unites closely to the divine mind. So you will be disposed to accept truth by revelation.

You will not accept it blindly or without question. You must criticize, evaluate, sift and examine. But in the end it will be unreasonable to claim that God has left the world without any knowledge of God's nature and purposes, or any hope of closer knowledge of God. Only God could provide such knowledge. Revelation becomes a highly probable consequence of the existence of a supremely good God. Perhaps that is why Dawkins and friends are so resolutely opposed to the God hypothesis.

Part 2: The Sense of the Infinite

Visions and voices are not the main or most frequent sorts of personal experience of God. The chief mark of a religious sensibility is well portrayed by William Blake when he speaks of holding 'infinity in the palm of your hand, and eternity in an hour'.[4] The religious sensibility is the apprehension of a deeper reality known in and through some finite reality, and conveying a sense of overwhelming value and power.

Such a sense can be conveyed by the beauties of the natural world, by the elegance and complexity of physical structures, and by great works of art, literature and music. It may be called a 'sense of transcendence', of beauty, power and goodness, which communicates an apprehension of a reality underlying the appearance of space, time and sense.

A faint analogy to this is the way in which we can take a person's expression or gestures as communicating what is in their mind. We then take the physical as a manifestation of a (to us) hidden mental reality of thought and feeling. But this is not the source of the sense of transcendence; it is just something vaguely like it.

The sense of transcendence is the sense that the visual, tactile and aural impressions that tell us of the nature of a hidden world of quarks and atoms also tell us of a spiritual reality of beauty and power which those impressions express in a fragmentary way. The impressions are 'sacraments', or sensory signs, of the reality of Spirit on which they ultimately depend.

Spirit, in other words, is not just a postulate of reason. It is apprehended in every experience that we have, so that every experience, rightly seen, is an encounter with Spirit, with eternal reality apprehended under the forms of time.

Dawkins says, 'If there is a logical argument linking the existence of great art to the existence of God, it is not spelled out by its proponents.'[5] The argument is not that if there is great art there must be a God to account for it; that would indeed be silly. The argument is that if there is a supreme Spirit, it will be known through works of beauty that express part of its nature in a striking and effective way. As composers, artists and writers find an affinity with the creative power of Spirit, they may be able to generate works of sublime beauty and significance that evoke apprehensions of transcendence as it has been mediated through their unique and particular perspectives.

Great art does not prove God. It expresses transcendent Spirit, and that is what links art to the existence of God. Many people will fail to see this. One reason is that they may, like Dawkins, believe in all conscience that the idea of God is incoherent, improbable and harmful. That makes any perception of God in nature, art and science virtually impossible. The natural awe and wonder that Dawkins feels before our amazing universe will have to be ascribed to something other than God.

Yet there is natural awe and wonder. And if God could be seen as highly probable, deeply rational and supremely valuable, then God would be the most appropriate object for those feelings. A theist would see such feelings of non-believers as apprehensions of God, the true character of which is misinterpreted. I have no wish to annoy Dawkins by saying this. But, just as he must see my belief in God as a delusion, so I must see his atheism as a sort of blindness, a failure to see what is there, a misinterpretation of experience.

Apprehensions of transcendence can exist in varying degrees – some people feel them constantly and intensely, others only occasionally, and some not at all, apparently. They are also interpreted in very diverse ways – Buddhists will not ascribe them to a supreme Spirit, while Hindus and Christians may give different interpretations of the supreme Spirit they are supposed to be expressing.

Sometimes this is taken as an objection to the veracity of a sense of transcendence. If some people apprehend Jahweh, and others apprehend Krishna, surely these claims are contradictory, and so they destroy each other? It is easy to see that this is not the case. The differences are in contrasting conceptual interpretations of the basic experience. The differences depend on varying philosophical starting-points, or assessments of the probability of God or of specific claims to revealed knowledge of God. The experiences themselves are vague and unspecific enough to be interpreted in a number of different ways. What is common to them is the sense of beauty, power and goodness, of eternity and infinite reality, mediated in various ways.

So when the theologian Friedrich Schleiermacher speaks of 'the sense of absolute dependence',[6] when Rudolf Otto speaks of the 'numinous' sense of mystery, awe and love,[7] and when the Jewish scholar Martin Buber speaks of an 'I–Thou' encounter with objects of human awareness,[8] these are different ways of seeking to describe, always inadequately, a basic experience of transcendence.

The sense of the infinite, of an unbounded reality of supreme beauty and goodness mediated through finite experiences, is not an independent proof of a specific kind of God. It is the experiential confirmation of a rational postulate about ultimate reality – one that I have defended as the God hypothesis. It is also, for many people, an experience impressive enough to lead them to renounce reductive materialism, and seek a more spiritual interpretation of the reality they seem to encounter in their own lives.

Schleiermacher, one of the great analysts of personal religious experience, said: 'To be one with the infinite in the midst of the finite and to be eternal in a moment, that is the immortality of religion.'[9] This may not be a complete definition of religion. But if anyone lacks this sense, or fails to feel its power, then, and only then, we can say that they are genuinely atheists. And their world, I believe, will be the poorer.

Part 3: The Path of Self-Transcendence

Belief in God is not just about having experiences of transcendence, though it is partly that. It is about personal commitment to a practice of self-transcendence. The believer is someone who thinks that there is just one ultimate reality of supreme beauty, bliss and goodness, and that finite intelligences in the cosmos exist in order to share in that beauty, bliss and goodness. Just as the test of genuine belief that smoking is bad for you is whether or not you smoke, so the test of genuine belief in God is whether or not your life is directed towards sharing in and learning to increase in the world around you beauty, bliss and goodness.

This is why belief in God is often called 'faith', and not just intellectual assent. Faith is the practical commitment to a relationship with God that will progressively transform your life, liberating it from hatred, greed and ignorance, and enabling it to become a more effective mediator of transcendent beauty, joy, compassion and benevolence.

Many of Dawkins' objections to religious belief are that he cannot see that religious believers are like that. He finds them, apparently, to be blind, unquestioning, slaves of obtuse authorities, hypocritical, prejudiced and repressive. Perhaps that is because they are human, after all. He is absolutely right to criticize any forms of religion that cause people to be like that. But if there is a God, we just have to live with that fact. It does not seem correct, or even sensible, to say that God, the ultimate reality of supreme value, is harmful. What we need to do is find some way of getting people really to believe in this God, and to act in appropriate and non-harmful ways.

That is extremely difficult. Human beings, whether they are religious or not, seem to be locked into a social world of hatred, greed and ignorance. They want what they cannot have, or when they have it they no longer want it. They resent the good fortune of others, and take their own good fortune as a right. They are slaves to desire and prisoners of despair. They live in a world estranged from God, because they follow the path of selfishness and have turned away from the path of selfless action for the sake of good alone.

If this is true – and I admit it sounds very pessimistic, though human history regrettably seems to support it – just getting such people to be religious is not magically going to make everything better. All it will do is make religion worse. In other words, we should expect religions to be full of selfish, spiteful, ambitious and ignorant people. We should not be surprised at that, because it is such people that religion wants to get hold of – and having got hold of them, it has to live with them.

Of course, religions want to connect people with God, they want to make people into mediators of supreme beauty, wisdom, compassion and bliss. But you have to accept that the whole thing is going to get corrupted – not fatally, but badly enough to be very uncomfortable. That is no excuse for bad and harmful religion. But it is an explanation of why it is that there are so many frauds and hypocrites in religion. Religions exist largely to increase wisdom, compassion and joy, and to liberate humans from self-obsessive desire. But they only partly succeed, and the failures, while very apparent, should not be allowed to obscure the goal.

In our world, the first stage in coming to know God, as objective Ideal, is likely to be a lively awareness of human moral ineptitude, and of the unsatisfactoriness of an ordinary life of conflict and ambition. This may be coupled with a sense of the categorical and morally irresistible claim of obligation. As Jean Paul Sartre, once the apostle of total human freedom, said (in an interview on French television), he ceased being a radical existentialist when he realized that he was not free to kick a starving beggar in an Algerian street. There was an objective claim on his humanity.

That sense of moral claim does not have to be interpreted in a religious sense. Sartre was able to give it a Marxist interpretation, of a rather idiosyncratic sort. There is morality and obligation without belief in God – thank God! Yet the sense of absolute and objective obligation is hard to account for in a purely materialist philosophy. Where are those obligations supposed to be? It hardly seems good enough to say, as E. O. Wilson once did, that they are inclinations genetically implanted in us because they were conducive to the survival of our remote ancestors.[10] And it seems fairly irrational to say that they are just obvious obligations, and that is that (this would sound suspiciously like the 'blind faith' that Dawkins disparages so much in religion).

We could appeal, as Dawkins and David Hume do, to natural human sympathy and compassion. I fervently hope that works. But, Dawkins says, such feelings are rooted in things like a hope for repayment of favours given, and for acquiring a reputation for generosity.[11] They are the result of 'Darwinian mistakes', 'the misfired consequence of ancestral village life'.[12]

If I thought that, and if I was able to escape the tyranny of the genes, the 'selfish replicators', I would seek to escape such past mistakes, and pursue a more reasonable policy of enlightened self-interest – looking good, but quietly stashing away a tidy pile for myself. That would seem to me a perfectly rational policy. I would not suddenly go around committing robbery, rape and murder, because through no fault of my own I have been well brought up. But I would not hesitate to indulge in petty acts of dishonesty, deceit and financial 'juggling'. Sincere belief in God can make a difference to moral attitudes.

I would not suggest that God is necessary for morality. I hope that the practical claims of duty are strong enough to take precedence over any lack of intellectual belief in objective moral truths. But I do suggest that moral experience is an important root of belief in a God, and that, conversely, belief in God adds a particular strength and tone to the experience of obligation.

It does so in two main ways. First, if there is a God with a purpose for human life, and if that purpose is for humans to grow in wisdom, compassion and generosity, then it is fully intelligible to say that there is an objective obligation to be wise, compassionate and generous, whatever we may happen to feel. We do not invent our moral duties, or let them depend on the vagaries of past evolutionary success or on the contingencies of our present desires. The call to wisdom and compassion is the voice of God, and it commands categorically and authoritatively, though it may not speak to us in words.

Second, if God is an Ideal of supreme beauty and goodness, then we will not see our duties simply as the commands of some arbitrary power. We will rationally desire to know and love that supreme beauty, so that it may attract us to itself and shape our natures more fully on its own. The motivation for moral action will not just be duty; it will be love of the Good, and desire to be as like it, and to be as closely united with it, as we can.

The way a believer in God sees moral life is different from the way in which an unbeliever sees it. There are many ways in which morality can be seen, and they will make a difference to how we live. Theists see it as a set of objective and binding obligations, to be obeyed because they issue from a being of supreme beauty and wisdom, who alone of all things is worthy to be loved in an unqualified way.

When the moral life is seen in this way, it becomes a powerful testimony to the presence and activity of God. For God does not only command. God is, in Matthew Arnold's words, 'a higher power making for righteousness', and divine love and wisdom can empower and help our own efforts after greater justice and altruism. Further, though the presence of God is felt in judgment of our failures to love, it is also felt in forgiveness, as we feel remorse and resolve to begin again. Such feelings of judgment, forgiveness and empowerment are centrally important personal experiences that can give a continuing sense of the dynamic presence of God in human lives.

Finally, if there is a God, then moral endeavour will not be in vain. Such endeavour may often entail self-sacrifice or even martyrdom in the cause of justice. A creator God who creates in order that goodness may flourish will ensure that justice will be victorious, and will not be defeated through human failure or death. This is not mere 'pie in the sky', but a logical consequence of believing in a good and powerful creator. It means that moral effort will never be in vain, even if its consequences are not what we immediately expect or hope. It means that there will be a life beyond this-worldly death, that there will be judgment, and the possibility of forgiveness and fulfilment.

This was Immanuel Kant's major argument for God. He placed little reliance on purely theoretical arguments inferring to a necessary being. But he thought that practical commitment to the objectivity and supreme authority of morality entailed, for any rational agent, belief that vice and virtue would meet with their just rewards; that there would be, as he put it, 'happiness-in-accordance-with-virtue', which in turn entailed the postulation of a God who could ensure it.[13]

Kant's argument has been much derided. It is often said that, on Kant's own principles, you should simply do your duty for its own sake, in which case you need no appeal to after-life rewards. But I think there is more to it than that, though perhaps Kant did not state it very well.

The sort of moral commitment that consists in extirpating selfish desire and aiming at knowledge of, and perhaps even union with, a non-physical reality of supreme goodness is already a commitment to seeing the true self as at least potentially one with the Self of All. Immortality consists in such an overcoming of the selfish ego that we are able to identify wholly with the Supreme Self, which is beyond time. That is the immortality entailed by this distinctive sort of moral commitment. It is not just 'doing duty for its own sake' – possibly a very Prussian eighteenth-century sentiment, after all. It is seeing the moral life as one of affinity with a higher reality of wisdom, joy and compassion. If that is attained, there is indeed no selfish desire left, however enlightened. But maybe in our experience we come to realize that our journey towards it has hardly yet begun. More is possible and desirable, and if there is a God, there will be more. There will be the possibility of an ultimate fulfilment of life in God.

Thus a specific sort of attitude to the moral life, a sense of moral inadequacy, of absolute moral obligation, of a compassionate and co-operative moral presence and power, of judgment and forgiveness, and of liberation from the desiring self, can be a powerful confirmation of the existence of a morally purposing creator. You can be, and should be, a person of strong moral principle without belief in God. But there is a way of seeing morality that is virtually already a form of belief in transcendent moral goodness. And for many people, a serious commitment to the moral life will lead to that path. For the believer in God, morality and religion are indissolubly tied together, and morality, seen in this way, is itself a journey into God.

Part 4: Christian Experience of Christ and the Spirit

In this book I am not discussing the topic of revealed religion, or defending the Christian faith specifically. I am concerned with general reasons for believing in God, or for accepting the God hypothesis. Those reasons hold good for any theist, Jewish, Christian, Muslim, Hindu or Sikh (I apologize to all the religions

I have not mentioned). But it would be dishonest of me not to mention one sort of personal experience that is very important to me, and to Christians generally. Members of other faiths will be able to think of similar experiences within their own traditions, but at this point I will just spend a little time on the strength of specifically Christian personal experience.

The Christian faith would never have got started if there had not been an initial belief in real, objective appearances of Jesus from the world beyond the grave. Some Christians still have such visions of Jesus. But the vast majority of Christians do not. We Christians would still say, however, that we experience 'the living Jesus Christ'. This is not usually a matter of visions or voices. It is rather that we feel a real spiritual presence and power, other than ourselves, whose nature and character is described and defined by the Gospel records of the life of Jesus, and is amplified by New Testament accounts of encounters with the Spirit of Jesus in the early church.

For many Christians, reading the life of Jesus, or hearing that life reflected on in sermons, evokes a lively sense of our own inability to live as fully, as joyfully, and as lovingly as we should. The teachings of Jesus reveal all too clearly our hypocrisy, self-deceit and egoism. The death of Jesus on the cross shows what these things lead to. But it also shows the lengths to which God goes to forgive us. The resurrection of Jesus from death shows that the power of the divine love that filled his life still exists, and is never defeated by suffering and death.

This can lead us to respond to the message of Christ by dying to our old selves of hatred and despair, as Christ died on the cross, and seeking to live again in the power of his resurrection life. A fundamental Christian experience is that of dying to self and being raised to new life through an active power of reconciliation and love, that comes to us as we turn from self to Christ, through whom the wisdom and power of God comes to us.

The daily experience of Christians is one of following the

way of the cross, so that we learn to give ourselves as Christ gave himself out of love for us. And it is one of living in the power of the resurrection, as the Spirit acts within us to embrace us in a wider life and deeper love.

Christians seek to live so that they can say, with St Paul, 'It is not I who live, but Christ who lives in me' (Galatians 2:20). The point about this experience is that it is not felt as a mood or an emotion that we conjure up in ourselves. It is felt as a response to the forgiving and renewing power of God that comes through the preaching of the good news of Jesus, and in the offer of his life in the bread and wine of the Eucharist.

Of course, if you do not believe in God at all, you will discount such experiences – though they often take people by surprise, and lead them to see that the God hypothesis is not so absurd after all. But, just as the best evidence that someone loves you is that they meet and embrace you, so the best evidence that God exists and desires your welfare is that God, in Jesus, gave the divine life *for* you, and that this same God, in the Spirit, gives the divine life *to* you, to raise you to a more joyful, fuller life.

Such a vivid personal experience is not given to all Christians – though it may be a fundamental feature of much Christian experience in a not fully conscious, not so vivid and intensely felt, but nevertheless significant, way. It seems to be the case, for whatever reasons of psychology or social convention, that a vivid experience of conversion and sanctification is only felt by a sizeable minority of Christians. Yet it is not entirely plausible to say that a large number of psychologically healthy and morally altruistic people are suffering from some sort of delusion. It is more plausible to think that the majority of people are unable to experience what is truly there, for a variety of reasons ranging from simply not being neurologically suited for such experiences to an active aversion to religion.

If you are thinking seriously about the God hypothesis, it will be very strong evidence if a large number of people, apparently well-balanced, intelligent and virtuous, feel that God has met them in the proclamation of Christ's teaching, death and resurrection, and has transformed their lives for the better through a sense of the presence of the Spirit of Christ in their lives. It would be reasonable to trust their testimony, and to embark on a way of life that has a chance of leading to a personal sense that there is a God who will wipe away all tears and lead us to an eternal and indestructible good.

8

Why There Is a God

Why There Almost Certainly Is a God

I can see how, for Dawkins, all this must seem like a wish-fulfilling fantasy. I can see how he feels compelled to call for cold, hard honesty rather than such illusory comfort. Where is the evidence for such dreams? Why does there seem not to be enough to convince us all?

As to the question of evidence, I think that is rather like asking why we have to try so hard to discover scientific truth. Why did God not just tell us about quantum physics, and make it all obvious? There is a truth about the physical world, but it is extremely hard to discover. Part of being human is having to learn for ourselves, after taking many false paths and blind alleys, what the world is like.

In morality, too, we have to learn by experience, through argument and reflection – and even then there is no unanimity of opinion. So in questions of metaphysics, about the ultimate nature of reality, about human nature, and about the best way to live, we have to learn and argue and follow our own reason as well as we can.

The question of God is not a purely intellectual puzzle. It is bound up with the basic ways in which we see our lives, the cultural histories and traditions from which we spring and against which we often react, and the most fundamental values, feelings and commitments we have. It is not just a question of evidence, in the sense of clear public data that put matters beyond any reasonable doubt. It is a question of basic forms of perspective and action.

As a believer in God, I strongly feel that in such questions it is not a matter of all the good and wise people thinking there is a God, and all the bad and silly people thinking there is not (or vice versa). All of us have partial perspectives, and we need to engage with others to see what the limits and advantages of those perspectives are.

For me, Dawkins' perspective is very partial, since it omits important questions of consciousness, value and purpose that seem very obviously part of the human world. It seems to me to lack any sympathy with the idea of an objective Ideal of supreme goodness and beauty, towards which human life is orientated at its most basic level, and which is discernible in the intelligibility of the physical world, in the beauties of nature and art, in the demand and attraction of morality, and in the sense of personal presence that can be felt in prayer and contemplation.

I have said little about that last aspect, though it is in the end the most important. The practice of prayer and contemplation is simply the practice of seeking to be aware of the spiritual presence of God, and to become more able to mediate the perfections of God in a unique manner of our own. There is little of worth that can be achieved in this life without hard work and constant practice. Knowing God, and seeking to shape human lives to the divine perfections, needs such practice. Without it, it will hardly be surprising if little awareness of God is felt. But in contemplation the presence of God can suffuse the whole of life to such a degree that it is completely transformed, because it is united more closely to God. That is the final goal of faith, of practical commitment to the God hypothesis. Such faith can become so strong that it is almost impossible to understand how anyone else can fail to desire it. But it will not move those who, for whatever reason, distrust all alleged personal experiences of God.

I would absolutely not believe that people like Dawkins are in some way to be 'eternally punished' for what seems to me a bout of intellectual myopia. I do think, however, that he is missing something very important about the nature of reality, and that at some point and in some way he, and others like him, will need a widening of vision that will disclose the reality of God to him. How this will come it is not for me to say. But as a Christian I feel compelled to say that God will meet him with unlimited love and the offer of unconditional forgiveness. If there is a hell, it is a condition in which persons have knowingly rejected the clearly perceived love of God. Jesus taught Christians not to judge when this is true of anyone. And it seems clear that all Christians should pray that it will not, in the end, be true of anyone.

I cannot think that a God of supreme love would condemn anyone just for honestly not thinking that God exists. So, however God comes to be known to atheists, it will be in love and compassion, not in some paroxysm of vindictive glee, as if to say, 'There, I told you so; you should have believed, shouldn't you? But now it's too late. Hee hee.' Even if there are people who think that is what God is like, that cannot be what a God of supreme goodness is actually like. That is why believers in God should regard honest atheists with regret that atheists have no experience of such unconditional love, but still with due respect for whatever honesty and concern for truth and goodness they have, and with hope that such concern will lead them at last to acknowledge God.

I can understand that, to Dawkins, people like me – believers in God – are deluded, because we fail to see that all real things are material, that values are projections of purely human desires and preferences, and that all things spring from a few simple, elementary entities and rules of their regular interaction. Moreover, he identifies many dangerous and harmful religious practices that use God as a stick to increase guilt, repress original thought and generally keep people in ignorance of their real natures. And he positively values wonder at the physical world, honesty in its investigation and concern for truth at any cost in psychological discomfort.

These things I can understand. But it is harder to understand his hatred of virtually all belief in God, and his mistaken belief that he has shown God to be very, very improbable. In this short text I have shown that what he takes to be his strongest argument – the Boeing 747 gambit – basically misses the mark by failing entirely to take any account of consciousness and personal explanation. His treatment of the traditional arguments for God is unacceptably cursory, and shows total lack of sympathy with any philosophical position other than his own. And his own philosophical position, while it seems to be a form of materialism, is very unclear, and is a rather recent and highly controversial view among philosophers.

To counter his arguments, I have argued for the key role of consciousness, value and purpose in any reasonably comprehensive view of the universe we live in. I have shown that the traditional arguments for God express a concern to find a final explanation for the universe with which many modern scientists, especially cosmologists, are in great sympathy. And I have shown that the arguments from personal experience for God, the ones that move most people to believe in God, are entirely reasonable and convincing.

In fact, taken overall, it seems to me the evidence, considered critically and rationally, makes it almost certain that there is a God.

On Being Certain

Almost certain? Can I really mean that, when so many thousands of people do not believe there is a God, and when Dawkins and others argue so strongly against belief in God? Well, I mean it in the same sense that Dawkins means it when he says that there 'almost certainly is no God'.

He does not mean, he cannot mean, that it is confirmable beyond all reasonable doubt that there is no God. Just as there are thousands of atheists, so there are thousands of theists, and thousands of them are informed, rational, morally committed human beings. There is always room for reasonable doubt.

What he means, I think, is that a sure grasp of the astonishing progress of modern science suggests the truth of some version of materialism. If you are a materialist, then obviously the very idea of God, of an immaterial conscious being, is nonsense. That is why the Boeing 747 gambit is, for him, a statement of the obvious. All conscious beings are the product of very complicated material processes, and probably that is all that they are. That is why any argument from alleged personal experiences of God or spiritual beings is a non-starter, and they have to be seen as delusions. That is why it is not worth spending much time on the traditional arguments for God. Once you are a committed materialist, God has to be a delusion. For a materialist, it is indeed almost certain that there is no God – you have eliminated the possibility of God with your very first step.

But I am absolutely not a materialist. I think the progress of modern science, especially in quantum physics and cosmology, shows that the very concept of 'matter' as the ultimate basis of all reality is obscure and almost impossible to define. Physicists talk about space and time being dimensions that are interchangeable in certain circumstances and that are only four of many other dimensions. They talk about imaginary time as being more real than 'real time'. They talk about reality being composed of wave functions, about matter and energy being interchangeable, and about fields of force that balance and interact in complex, non-picturable but mathematically describable ways.

In addition, the attempts of some neuropsychologists and researchers into Artificial Intelligence to explain consciousness purely in material terms seem to deny the obvious facts of personal conscious experience and action, and to make very large, dogmatic and highly speculative claims about the future success of their disciplines. Cognitive psychology has largely ousted behaviourism and past attempts to see mental processes as irrelevant causal factors. And the hope that art, morality and culture will one day be in principle explicable in terms of physics is little more than a faith in the competence of physics that goes so far beyond the available evidence that it must be seen as a passionate commitment to a preferred world-view, a commitment made in conditions of objective uncertainty. (Incidentally, this is Søren Kierkegaard's definition of 'faith', though in this case it is clearly not a religious faith.)

Belief in God begins from a position more agnostic and open-minded than this. It allows for the possibility that the facts of consciousness and purpose of which we are so directly aware in our own experience of the world may be of fundamental importance in the universe as a whole. The God hypothesis explores the possibility that consciousness and purpose may be at the heart of objective reality. It does so in various ways, and with various degrees of tentativeness and temerity.

As I have presented the case, there are two main avenues of exploration. One leads to the search for a final explanation of the cosmos. The other leads to a consideration of various types of personal experience that suggest a sense of transcendent value. I have suggested that in both cases the God hypothesis succeeds in providing a unifying postulate that underpins a sophisticated intellectually, morally and psychologically satisfying way of living in the world.

It seems to me that it easily trumps the materialist world-view, being truer to the rich variety of human experience, and much better able to account for the deep sense of objective beauty, intelligibility and goodness that drives and sustains so much of human endeavour – including the best sort of scientific endeavour. But in the end, after all these considerations, it is a whole-hearted commitment to a way of life that is centred on love of the good and beautiful that makes the existence of God virtually certain.

This is not a dispassionate theoretical certainty that allows no rational opposition. It is a practical certainty that involves the whole person in a form of life, the force of which comes to seem utterly compelling. It is from this perspective that there is almost certainly a God.

So do we have two certainties in direct conflict with one another? Yes, and more than two, though the others are not my concern here! The sense of paradox is eased when a clear distinction is made between theoretical and practical certainty, and when you see that some of the things you take to be theoretically certain are only so given the prior adoption of a more basic claim that is not theoretically certain. It is because Dawkins is a materialist that he is certain there is no God. It is because I am an idealist (in the very broad sense of accepting consciousness or mind as the fundamental character of reality) that I am certain there is a God.

In showing why we are certain about these things, we each have to elucidate the considerations that lead to the adoption of materialism and idealism respectively. At this level there is no theoretical certainty, and we each have to draw on a wide set of considerations and seek to place them in the perspective that seems most adequate to us.

I believe that I have conclusively shown Dawkins' arguments against God to fail, and I have shown also that his certainty that there is no God depends on a materialist world-view that is far from theoretically certain.

Idealism, too, is not theoretically certain. But if it is adopted, even as a living possibility, it can justify a practical certainty, and even a second-order theoretical certainty (a theoretical certainty, given the truth of idealism) of the existence of God.

It is not that both theism and atheism are equally reasonable. One of them is reasonable and true, and the other is not. The problem is that we cannot be sure which one is wrong. Rationality and truth are very hard to achieve. In this situation, I would say that both Dawkins and I are justified in being (practically) certain of the belief we hold, and we are both obligated to demonstrate the superiority of our own view if we can do so. I think I have done that – but then I would, wouldn't I?

Believing in God for Good Reasons

Those who believe in God for good reasons will be those who believe that the universe is rational and intelligible, and who are concerned for the trustworthiness of human reason; those who think that consciousness is a kind of reality that is inexplicable in purely physical terms, and that it is a fundamental and irreducible element of reality; those who think that its emergence in animals from a long process of increasing physical complexity and organization requires explanation in terms of an envisaged goal and intention; those who have some experience of transcendent value in beauty and in morality; those who feel the attraction of an Ideal of truth, beauty and goodness, which is objective and authoritative; and those who wish to penetrate in thought beyond sensory appearances to the hidden reality that lies beneath.

They will not be mad or deluded, blindly accepting of any human authority or uncritical of any passing fashion of human thought. They will seek to know the best that can be thought, and aim to imitate it insofar as they can in their own lives. They will be lovers of truth and beauty, and they may even feel themselves to be – and may in truth be, as far as humans ever can – beloved of God and sharers in divine immortality. This is the life above all others that humans should live. For if theists are right, it is in the contemplation of truth, beauty and goodness, both in themselves and in all their manifold finite forms, that humanity finds its highest fulfilment and happiness. And that will be humanity's highest truth – a life fulfilled in the knowledge and love of the supremely beautiful and good reality that theists call God.

Endnotes

Chapter 1

1. Richard Dawkins, *The God Delusion*, Bantam Press, 2006, p. 31.

2. *Ibid.*, p. 31.

3. *Ibid.*, p. 31.

4. Paul Davies and John Gribbin, *The Matter Myth,* Harmondsworth, Penguin, 1992.

5. Bernard d'Espagnat, *Reality and the Physicist*, Cambridge University Press, 1990.

6. Roger Penrose, *The Large, the Small and the Human Mind*, Cambridge University Press, 1997, p. 175.

7. Daniel Dennett, *Consciousness Explained,* New York, Penguin, 1992.

8. Richard Dawkins, *op. cit.*, p. 31, my emphases.

9. *Ibid.*, p. 38.

10. Richard Swinburne, *The Existence of God*, Oxford University Press, 2004, pp. 35–45.

11. Richard Dawkins, *op. cit.*, p. 150.

12. *Ibid.*, p. 73.

13. *Ibid.*, p. 50.

14. *Ibid.*, p. 59.

15. *Ibid.*, p. 61.

Chapter 2

1. Richard Dawkins, *The God Delusion*, p. 157.

2. *Ibid.*, p. 107.

3. *Ibid.*, p. 121.

4. *Ibid.*, p. 109.

5. Matt Ridley, *Genome*, London, Harper, 1999, p. 9.

6. Stephen J. Gould, *Wonderful Life*, New York, W.W. Norton, 1989.

7. Simon Conway Morris, *Life's Solution*, Cambridge University Press, 2003.

8. Richard Dawkins, *The Blind Watchmaker,* Penguin, 1991, Chapter 3.

9. Charles Darwin, *Origin of Species*, London, John Murray, 1859, p. 80.

10. *The Correspondence of Charles Darwin*, ed. Frederick Burkhardt and Sydney Smith, Cambridge University Press, 1985, vol. 8, p. 275.

11. Richard Dawkins, *The God Delusion,* p. 140.

12. *Ibid.*, p. 120.

13. *Ibid.*, p. 147.

14. *Ibid.*, p. 121.

15. *Ibid.*, p. 73.

16. *Ibid.*, p. 150.

Chapter 3

1. Richard Dawkins, *The God Delusion*, 147.

2. Eugene Wigner, 'The Unreasonable Effectiveness of Mathematics in Natural Sciences', *Communications in Pure and Applied Mathematics* vol. 13, February, 1960.

3. Martin Rees, *Our Cosmic Habitat*, Princeton University Press, 2001, p. 162.

4. Richard Dawkins, *op. cit.*, p. 126.

5. *Ibid.*, p. 132.

6. *Ibid.*, p. 31.

Chapter 4

1. An informative recent discussion, mostly from a strictly scientific point of view, is: Bernard Carr (ed.), *Universe or Multiverse?*, Cambridge University Press, 2007.

2. Lee Smolin, *The Life of the Cosmos*, New York, Oxford University Press, 1997.

3. Richard Dawkins, *The God Delusion*, p. 144.

4. Stephen Hawking, *A Brief History of Time,* 10th edition, 1998, p. 190.

5. George Ellis, 'Multiverses' in *Universe or Multiverse?*

6. Max Tegmark, 'The Multiverse Hierarchy' in *Universe or Multiverse?*

7. Alvin Plantinga, *The Nature of Necessity*, Oxford, Clarendon Press, 1974.

Chapter 5

1. Anselm, *Proslogion*, Chapter 2.

2. Steven Weinberg, *Dreams of a Final Theory*, London, Vintage, 1993, p. 191.

3. Albert Einstein, *Festchrift fur Aunel Stadola*, Zurich, Orell Fussli, p. 126.

4. Thomas Aquinas, *Summa Theologiae*, Part 1a, Question 25, Article 6.

5. Richard Dawkins, *The God Delusion*, p. 155.

6. *Ibid.*, p. 150.

7. Richard Taylor, *Action and Purpose*, New Jersey, Englewood Cliffs, 1966.

8. Richard Dawkins, *op. cit.*, p. 155.

9. *Ibid.*, p. 109.

Chapter 6

1. Thomas Aquinas, *Summa Theologiae*, Part 1a, Question 2, Article 3, 'Is There a God?'

2. Richard Dawkins, *The God Delusion*, p. 77.

3. Peter Atkins, *Creation Revisited,* Oxford, W. H. Freeman, 1992.

4. Immanuel Kant, *Critique of Pure Reason*, Transcendental Dialectic, Book 2, Chapter 3, 'The Ideal of Pure Reason'. See especially sections 3–5.

5. David Hume, *Dialogues Concerning Natural Religion*, Part 9.

6. David Hume, *An Inquiry Concerning Human Understanding*, section 1.

7. *Ibid.*, section 4, part 1.

8. Richard Dawkins, *op. cit.*, p. 78.

9. *Ibid.*, p. 57.

10. Plato, *Timaeus*, transl. Desmond Lee, Penguin, 1972, p. 50.

11. Richard Dawkins, *op. cit.*, p. 79.

12. Plato, *The Republic*, Book 10, 597.

13. Richard Dawkins, *op. cit.*, p. 79.

14. Aristotle, *Metaphysics*, Book 12.

15. Gottfried Leibniz, *Monadology*, paragraph 58.

16. Richard Dawkins, *The Selfish Gene*, Oxford University Press, 1976, p. 215.

17. Richard Dawkins, *The God Delusion*, p. 77.

18. Thomas Aquinas, *op. cit.* Part 1a, Question 2, Article 1.

19. Anselm, *Proslogion*, Chapter 2.

20. Immanuel Kant, *op. cit.*, Transcendental Dialectic, Chapter 3, section 3.

Chapter 7

1. Richard Dawkins, *The God Delusion*, p. 88.

2. *Ibid.*, p. 92.

3. *Ibid.*, p. 99.

4. William Blake, *Auguries of Innocence,* 1803.

5. Richard Dawkins, *op. cit.*, p. 87.

6. Friedrich Schleiermacher, *The Christian Faith*, trans. H. R. MacKintosh and J. S. Stewart, Edinburgh, T. & T. Clark, 1989, paragraph 4.

7. Rudolf Otto, *The Idea of the Holy*, trans. John Harvey, Penguin, 1959.

8. Martin Buber, *I and Thou*, trans. Ronald Gregor Smith, Edinburgh, T. & T. Clark, 1958.

9. Friedrich Schleiermacher, Fourth Speech from *On Religion*, trans. Richard Crouter, Cambridge University Press, 1988, originally published in German in 1799.

10. E. O. Wilson, *Consilience*, London, Little Brown, 1998, Chapter 11.

11. Richard Dawkins, *op. cit.*, p. 220.

12. *Ibid, op. cit.*, p. 222.

13. Immanuel Kant, *Critique of Practical Reason*, trans. L. W. Beck, New York, Bobbs-Merrill, 1956, *Dialectic of Pure Practical Reason*, originally published in German in 1788.

Further Reading

This is a small selection of books, in addition to those mentioned in the text, that provides further reading on the main themes of this volume.

On general religious or philosophical replies to the work of Richard Dawkins:

John Lennox, *God's Undertaker* (Lion, 2007).

Alister McGrath, *Dawkins' God* (Blackwell, 2005).

Alister McGrath, *The Dawkins Delusion* (Blackwell, 2007).

Keith Ward, *God, Chance and Necessity* (Oneworld, 1996).

On the general relation of science and religion:

Ian Barbour, *Religion and Science* (SCM 1998).

Kitty Ferguson, *The Fire in the Equations* (Bantam 1994).

Arthur Peacocke, *Creation and the World of Science* (Oxford, Clarendon, 1979).

Arthur Peacocke, *Paths from Science towards God* (Oneworld, 2001).

John Polkinghorne, *One World* (SPCK 1986).

John Polkinghorne, *Science and Creation* (SPCK 1988).

John Polkinghorne, *Science and Providence* (SPCK 1989).

Keith Ward, *Pascal's Fire* (Oneworld, 2006).

Keith Ward, *The Big Questions in Science and Religion* (Templeton Foundation Press, 2008).

For a readable, scholarly and unbiased account of Western philosophy:

Anthony Kenny, *A Brief History of Western Philosophy* (Blackwell, 1998).

On personal explanation and the problem of consciousness:

Richard Swinburne, *The Existence of God*, especially chapter two (Oxford, Clarendon, 2004).

Charles Taliaferro, *Consciousness and the Mind of God* (Cambridge University Press, 1994).

Keith Ward, *Religion and Human Nature*, especially chapter seven (Clarendon, 1998).

On interpreting the Old Testament:

Bernhard Anderson, *The Living World of the Old Testament* (Longman, 1980).

On anthropic and fine-tuning arguments:

Michael Denton, *Nature's Destiny* (Free Press, 1998).

John Leslie, *Universes* (Routledge, 1989).

Neil Manson (ed.) *God and Design: the Teleological Argument and Modern Science* (Routledge, 2003).

On the concept of God:

Keith Ward, *Religion and Creation*, especially Part Three (Clarendon, 1996).

Keith Ward, *God, a Guide for the Perplexed* (Oneworld, 2002).

A. N. Whitehead, *Process and Reality,* final chapter (Macmillan, 1978).

Arguments for God:

J. Houston (ed.) *Is it Reasonable to Believe in God?* (Edinburgh, Handsel Press, 1984).

E. L. Mascall, *He Who Is* (Darton, Longman, Todd, 1966).

Richard Swinburne, *The Coherence of Theism* (OUP, 1977).

Richard Swinburne, *The Existence of God* (Oxford, Clarendon Press, 2004).

Keith Ward, *Rational Theology and the Creativity of God* (Blackwell, 1982).

On evil and the goodness of God:

John Hick, *Evil and the God of Love* (Harper and Row, 1966).

Marilyn McCord Adams, *Horrendous Evils and the Goodness of God* (Cornell University Press, 1999).

Alvin Plantinga, *God, Freedom and Evil* (Allen and Unwin, 1974).

David Ray Griffin, *God, Power, and Evil* (Westminster Press, 1976).

On revelation and religious experience:

William Alston, *Perceiving God* (Cornell University Press, 1991).

F. R. Tennant, *Philosophical Theology* (Cambridge University Press, 1928).

Keith Ward, *Religion and Revelation* (Clarendon, 1994).

Index